Dave Celentano's Guitar Techniques

Performance enhancing exercises designed to
increase accuracy, speed, agility,
and maximize practice time.

Cover photos – KLK Photography
Cover design – Shawn Brown
Music Notation – Dave Celentano

ISBN 1-57424-127-3
SAN 683-8022

INTRODUCTION

Having awesome technique alone doesn't make a great guitarist, there are other factors involved that complete the equation. In addition to technique, a good ear, sense of timing, and being able to read music are what truly make up a well rounded musician. However, technique is the link between your hands and the music that is ultimately heard. The term 'technique' is defined as the development of specific skills involved in playing an instrument (like hand and finger dexterity, vibrato, hammer ons, pull offs, trills, and tapping) that enables the musician to perform the composition effortlessly. Developing *your* facilities to the point where you can perform whatever music you may hear in your head or desire to learn should be of utmost importance.

The exercises and technical studies contained in this volume serve as a good starting point to build your technique and hone your chops. I've seen positive results in my students when they used these exercises to work on specific weak areas. No matter what level of proficiency you are on the guitar, you'll find something new and challenging in this book. As an added bonus the accompanying audio CD contains a song I wrote called "World Music Jam" (track 73), followed by a jam along version of the same song (track 74) with no lead solos. A complete transcription of the song is included at the end of this volume.

There are no shortcuts on the road to becoming a great guitarist. You've got to put in the hours, days, weeks, and years of consistent practice. It takes dedication, discipline, and above all, a genuine love for your guitar.

-Dave Celentano

Acknowledgments

Thanks to World Music in Santa Clarita, Grayson's Tunetown, Ron Middlebrook, Ben Cole at GHS Strings, and all my students for giving me inspiration to write this book. Dave uses GHS Strings and Rocktron amplification.

Audio CD recorded and engineered at Yaking Cat Music Studios by Brandon Amison.
All guitars- Dave Celentano
Bass- Randy Landas
Drums- Bill Brennenstuhl

Photograph taken by Kevin Karzin

As a teenager, Dave Celentano received guitar lessons from fellow high school mate Marty Friedman (lead guitarist with Megadeth). Soon after, Dave attended G.I.T. (Guitar Institute of Technology) in Hollywood, where he studied the guitar under Jennifer Batten, Keith Wyatt, Frank Gambale, and Paul Gilbert. During his tenure at G.I.T. Dave began writing material for what would become his first book *The Magic Touch*, which was published when he was only twenty two years old. Since then he's written more than thirty educational guitar books, videos, and CDs for Centerstream Publications, Hal Leonard Corporation, and Star Licks Instructional videos. Some of Dave's best selling books for Centerstream include *Flying Fingers, Monster Scales and Modes, Essential Blues Guitar, Killer Pentatonics, Modal Jams and Theory, Speed Metal, Rock Around the Classics, Over the Top Tapping, Rockin' Christmas for Guitar,* and *Surf Guitar.* Dave also wrote and designed a six video course for Centerstream- *Beginning, Intermediate,* and *Advanced Rock Rhythm Guitar* and *Beginning, Intermediate,* and *Advanced Rock Lead Guitar,* encompassing all the essential tools to help build a solid foundation for lead and rhythm. In addition, he wrote columns and transcribed songs for Guitar School magazine, performed clinics in conjunction with GHS Strings at G.I.T. and music stores on the west coast, and released a CD with his progressive rock band 'Sir Real' in Japan. Most recently, Dave's worked with Hal Leonard Corporation by writing and performing on the *Signature Series Rod Stewart* book/CD and *Signature Series Allman Brothers* DVD. Currently, Dave's working on several new books, teaching private and group classes, and writing music for his new album.

All Dave Celentano's educational products can be ordered directly from Hal Leonard Corporation through your local music store or online at *musicdispatch.com*.

TABLE OF CONTENTS AND CD TRACK LIST

Definition Of Symbols

P = pull off

H = hammer on

SL = slide

T = tap with picking hand

① = circle around fingering indicates tap with picking hand

V = up stroke

∏ = down stroke

⋀⋁⋀ = vibrato

∕⁄. = repeat previous bar

PRACTICE

The best piece of advice regarding practice is to use this time to work on deficiencies in your guitar playing (we all have a few). A typical practice session for many guitarists is to jam on familiar songs or run through the same old scales, licks, and exercises. In moderation this is fine, but there must be a specific time set aside every time you sit down to practice for working on weak areas in your playing. Be honest and ask yourself "What aspects of my guitar playing need the most work?", "Can I change chords effectively without missing a beat?", "Am I consistently alternate picking when I should be?", "Do I know my scales in all keys?". These are just a few typical questions you should be asking yourself and, of course, the questions should pertain to the specific style and goals you wish to achieve. For instance, a classical guitarist might be more concerned with mastering finger picking rather than knowing the blues scale in all positions. Or a country guitarist would focus on hybrid picking (picking with the pick, middle, and ring fingers) instead on tapping (although it might be cool to do tapping in country).

There's no secret to becoming an accomplished guitarist, and the only way to get there is by putting in the practice time. In fact, I can't think of any decent guitarist who hasn't logged numerous hours in the woodshed. Guitar virtiousos like Yngwie Malmsteen, Edward Van Halen, Al Di Meola, John McLaughlin, John Petrucci, Paul Gilbert, Joe Satriani, Steve Vai, and Steve Morse all dedicated several hours every day for years to fine tune their craft and build chops. I believe that the great musicians are those that truely love there instrument, and when they are not with the instrument they are thinking about it.

You too can master the guitar, but you'll need a plan of action. A consistent practice regimen is the surest way to become proficient on the guitar, so let's consider some of the elements required for a productive practice session. First, find a quiet spot where you can give the guitar your undivided attention, then relax and clear your mind of all things except what you're about to practice. The session should include warming up with finger exercises and scales, working on techniques that are challenging you (hammer ons, pull offs, tapping, etc.), chords and rhythm work, and working with the metronome at various tempos. A two hour practice session six days a week is more productive than nothing all week and then pulling a few eight hour marathon sessions on the weekend. Even if all you can afford is thirty minutes a day, it's far more effective than waiting until you've got a bigger block of time. Develop a routine that fits your schedule and commit to it.

Maintain a clear vision of where you want your guitar playing to be in the future by setting goals. Ask yourself, "Where do I want my playing to be in one year?", then set short term goals that you can shoot for along the way. These short term goals are stepping stones towards achieving your ultimate goal. Imagine your one year goal is to be able to solo and improvise over a twelve bar blues progression. First, you must know how to play the blues scale in one key, so make it a short term goal to learn one of the five blues scale patterns each week. A monthly goal would be to learn and play the blues scale in two other keys as well. Next, try your hand at soloing over blues rhythm tracks in the key you're working on. At this point the scales must be memorized otherwise the soloing excursion could result in a train wreck since you don't know the correct notes by heart. Continue using small short term goals that lead you to your ultimate destination.

While growing up I would read about my favorite guitarists and discovered that many of them practiced four to ten hours a day. At that time my goal was to become a great player and I figured that if I practiced as much as my idols did I could reach my goal. Well, situations arose (work and other responsibilities in life) that prevented me from putting in those kind of hours, so I had to re-think my plan. Rather than noodling around and playing whatever I felt like for eight hours a day, I realized I could cut my practice time down to two or three hours a day by focusing on and practicing specific tasks in short ten to fifteen minute sessions.

Example of a typical two hour practice session:

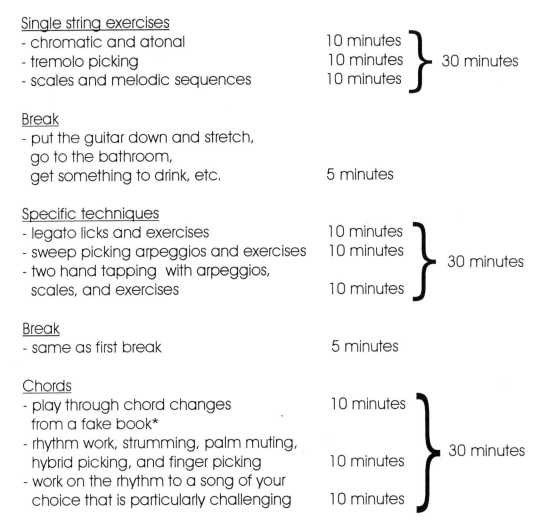

Single string exercises
- chromatic and atonal   10 minutes ⎫
- tremolo picking   10 minutes ⎬ 30 minutes
- scales and melodic sequences   10 minutes ⎭

Break
- put the guitar down and stretch,
  go to the bathroom,
  get something to drink, etc.   5 minutes

Specific techniques
- legato licks and exercises   10 minutes ⎫
- sweep picking arpeggios and exercises   10 minutes ⎬ 30 minutes
- two hand tapping with arpeggios,
  scales, and exercises   10 minutes ⎭

Break
- same as first break   5 minutes

Chords
- play through chord changes   10 minutes ⎫
  from a fake book*   ⎪
- rhythm work, strumming, palm muting,   ⎬ 30 minutes
  hybrid picking, and finger picking   10 minutes ⎪
- work on the rhythm to a song of your   ⎪
  choice that is particularly challenging   10 minutes ⎭

*This book is loaded with jazz standards using common and not so common chords and progressions, and is an invaluable source for all musicians. Even if you don't like jazz you'll benefit tremendously by learning these types of chords and songs.

Break
- same as first break   5 minutes

<u>Ear training</u>
- transcribe songs, and recognize intervals
  and chord qualities by ear   15 minutes

Transcribing songs by ear is the best way to improve your ear. This is how most guitarists learn. Begin with an easy song where the guitar is clearly defined and avoid songs with too many fast passages of notes (you can attempt the fast stuff later once your ear has developed). The elusive art of transcribing can take a while to master, but is well worth the time devoted to it. For more on transcribing check out my book "The Art Of Transcribing". Other ear training tools include recognizing and identifying intervals (minor 2nd, major 2nd, minor 3rd, major 3rd, perfect 4th, etc.) and chord qualities (major, minor, dominant, augmented, etc) by ear, that's without your guitar.

<u>Jamming and letting loose</u>
- Play songs you know
- Improvise   15 minutes

This is a time for letting it all hang out, having fun, and expressing yourself without strict guidelines. Play songs that are fun and try to be creative. Write a song using some of the new techniques you're learning.

In everything you play always be relaxed, maintain good posture, and think economy of finger motion. Use the smallest and most efficient finger movements to perform the piece of music. Make a habit of learning something new everyday that will make you a better guitarist. What and how you practice will directly effect your performance with the band. You can have you're look together, the best instrument and amp, and talk a big game, but if you haven't done your homework on the guitar it will show. There's no gadget you can buy that will make you a better player. The *only* way to get good is to *practice*.

Tuning Notes

Track 2 features the six tuning notes corresponding to the six strings on your guitar. Tune to these notes to match the rest of this CD.

Metronome

The metronome is requisite for playing fast, articulate and smooth lines, and more importantly, playing with the beat. First, without the metronome, work out any trouble spots in the music. Next, set the metronome to a slow tempo where you can play the music with no mistakes and steady with the beat. Once you can play accurately and evenly at the slow tempo, gradually increase tempo. This is crucial for developing an good sense of timing.

In everything you play strive for smooth and even picking and finger movements, and no choppy sounds. If you haven't spent enough time working on your timing with the metronome it will show. This is the difference between the pro and amateur.

Picking Techniques

The three most common forms of picking are *alternate picking* (consistent down-up-down-up strokes), *sweep* or *economy picking* (two or more consecutive down or up strokes), and *circular picking* (controlling the tip of the pick in the same manner as writing with the tip of a pencil, the fingers guide the pick in a circular motion).

Both hands should be relaxed at all times. Never hold the pick with a death grip. Hold it just hard enough to keep it between the fingers, adding a little more pressure for louder dynamics and less pressure for softer dynamics. For fast single note passages try playing with just the tippy tip of the pick. I also prefer to hold the pick at an angle (about 30 degrees) to the string, so the edge of the pick strikes the string rather than the flat face.

Tremolo Technique

Tremolo is the rapid repeating of a single note. When applied to a melody it gives the illusion of sustained notes. Guitarists in many genres have successfully incorporated tremolo picking in their music. Edward Van Halen's "Eruption" and "Little Guitars (intro)", surf guitarist Dick Dale's "Miserlou", and several other surf songs all tickled our ears with dazzling displays of tremolo picking. In fact, in the classical field there have been volumes of exercises and songs written and devoted to tremolo technique that are now part of the classical guitar lexicon.

While the technique is simple to understand, it's challenging to master. Tremolo is produced by rapidly alternate picking (down-up-down-up). A successful tremolo technique must have evenness and articulation, and should be practiced with a metronome. Use tiny down and up pick strokes while striving for consistency in pick attacks (down and up strokes should sound the same volume and the notes should be spaced evenly apart).

Devote at least ten minutes a day (every day) to working on and developing your tremolo technique and you'll see definite improvements in your picking in a short period.

These next four exercises guide you step by step through the process of learning, developing, and mastering tremolo picking. The first (**track 3**) shows a simple melody on one string played as quarter notes using all down strokes.

Track 3

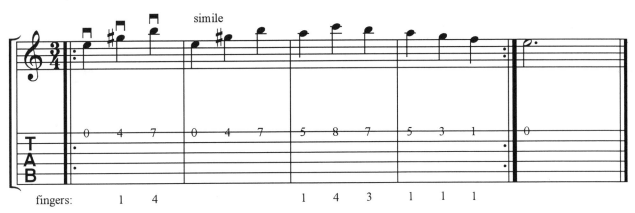

Next, pick each note twice as eighth notes using alternate picking (**track 4**).

Track 4

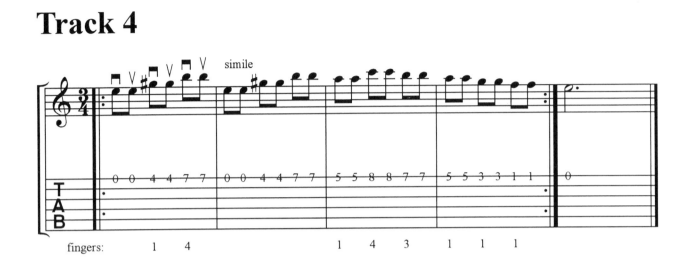

fingers: 1 4   1 4 3 1 1 1

Move up to sixteenth notes (**track 5**) by picking each note four times and twice as fast as eighth notes.

Track 5

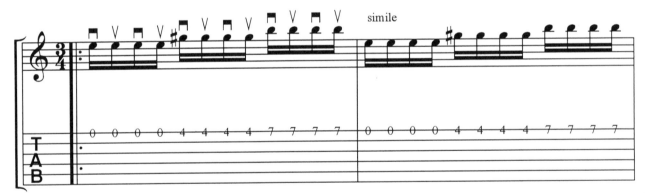

Finally, the true tremolo effect is achieved by picking ultra fast thirty-second notes (**track 6**). That's eight notes per beat! Make sure you're picking evenly and in time with the metronome.

Track 6

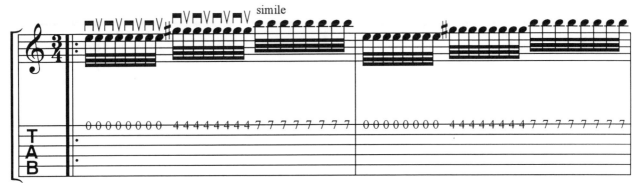

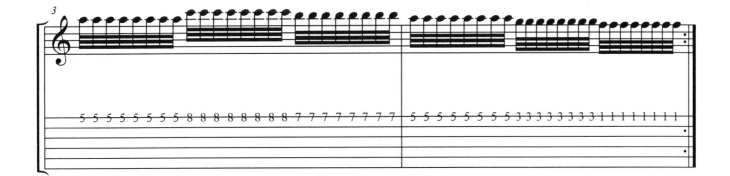

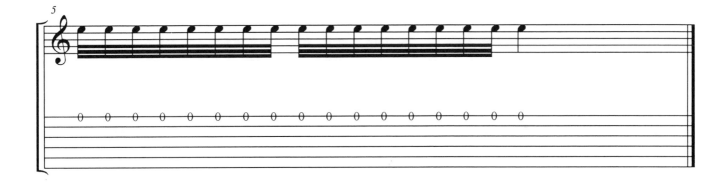

Below is an example of how tremolo is written in music notation.

How tremolo is notated

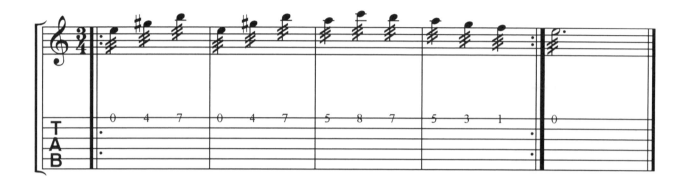

Now apply tremolo picking while crossing strings. **Track 7** is a Randy Rhoads style lick in A minor.

Track 7

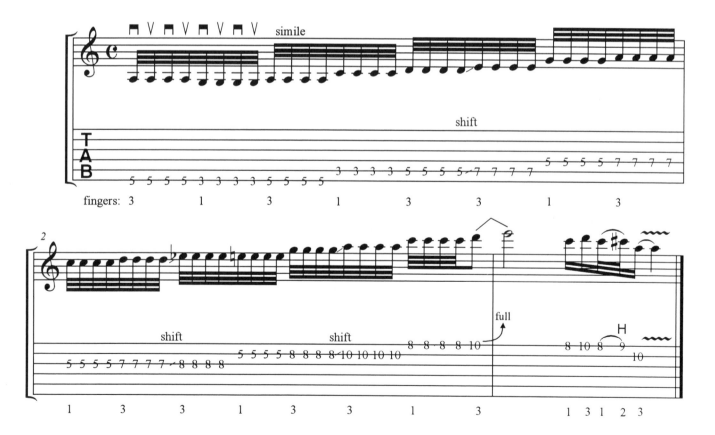

Finger Exercises

Warming up with exercises is a sure way to improve finger dexterity and avoid serious injuries like *carpal tunnel syndrome* and *tendonitis*. If you were going to run a 10k marathon you wouldn't just step up to the start line and take off- you'd stretch out and warm up first. You should develop a routine of exercises that use the essential bones, muscles, and tendons of both hands. The exercises in this volume are a good place to start. Each exercise develops specific techniques including alternate picking, finger independence and control, hammer ons, pull offs, trills, sweep picking, and string skipping.

A typical warm up should start out by playing *slowly* for the first ten minutes. Get the blood flowing and loosen up the muscles and tendons before letting it fly. Some of these exercises may sound cool, while some are down right dissonant. The point is to get the fingers moving, not make a musical statement.

When I first started playing guitar my instructor gave me an exercise that I found very practical (**track 8**). Soon I realized the workout developed finger independence, alternate picking, and most important, helped to synchronize both hands (which is requisite for playing guitar). Find a comfortable tempo where you can play steady and with no mistakes. It's pointless to play fast if it's sloppy and not in time.

Track 8

Track 9 is a variation that mixes up the fingers with an 'odd-even' pattern (fingers 1-3-2-4).

Track 9

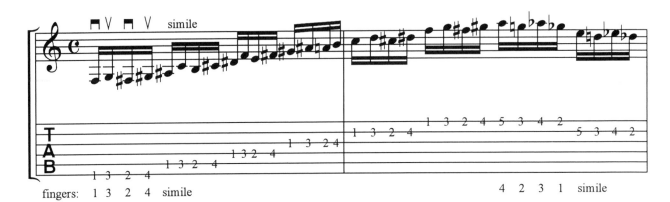

fingers: 1   3   2   4   simile   4   2   3   1   simile

I developed **track 10** to improve alternate picking while crossing strings. Notice the 'X' shape the fingers make on the fretboard.

Track 10

fingers: 1 2 3   4 3   2 3 2   1 2 3   4   simile

Around 1920 classical composer Arnold Schoenburg formulated the *twelve tone system* after rejecting the traditional tonal system. His atonal compositions using the twelve tone system had a huge influence on other composers of the twentieth century. Also known as the *twelve tone row* or *twelve tone technique*, the concept uses all twelve notes of the chromatic scale in a random order preselected by the composer, and no one note can by repeated until all eleven other notes are used. The challenge is to create an interesting melody while adhering to the rules of the twelve tone system. As you might imagine this method of writing produces some disturbingly dissonant melodies. The two sequences below (**track 11 and 12**) are unpredictable and particularly daring. The dissonance is augmented by the abundant use of *flat fifth* intervals.

Track 11

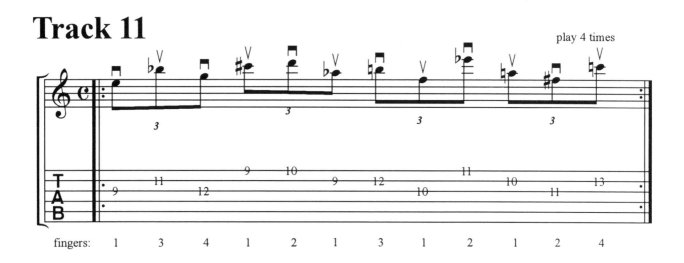

Track 12

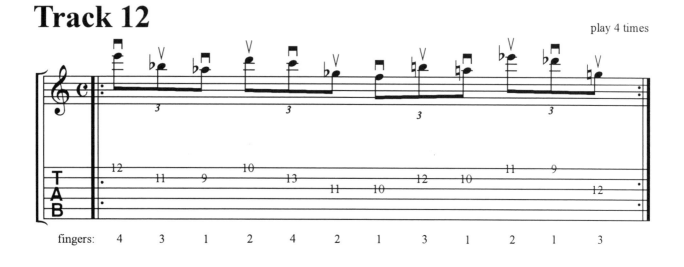

Another writing tool Schoenburg used was to play the sequence of notes in retrograde (in reverse order, read from right to left). Try playing the two previous examples in retrograde.

Diatonic Scale Exercises

There's no better way to get to know a scale than to ascend and descend with melodic sequences. These rudimentary patterns are moved through the scale diatonically, that means the established sequence of notes is moved up or down the scale using only scale tones. **Tracks 13, 14, and 15** use sequence groups of threes, fours, and sixes respectively. Start out slowly at first and don't forget to use strict alternate picking. For and added bonus try starting each example with an up stroke instead of a down.

Track 13

fingers: 1 2 4 2 4 1 4 1 2 1 2 4   etc.

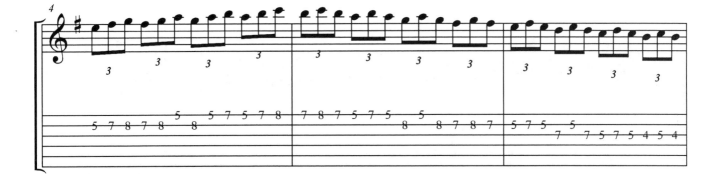

17

Track 14

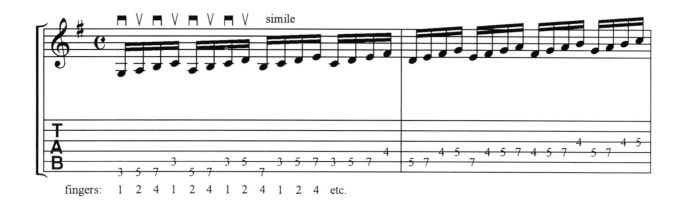

fingers: 1 2 4 1 2 4 1 2 4 1 2 4 etc.

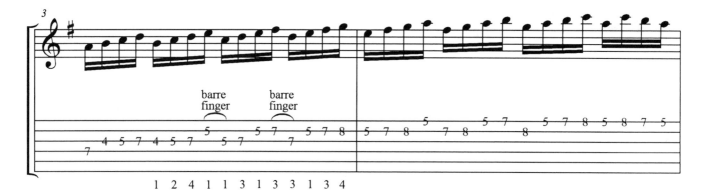

1 2 4 1 1 3 1 3 3 1 3 4

18

Track 15

fingers: 1 2 4 1 2 4 2 4 1 2 4 1 4 1 2 4 1 2 1 2 4 1 2 4 etc.

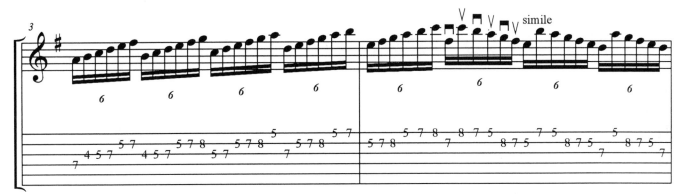

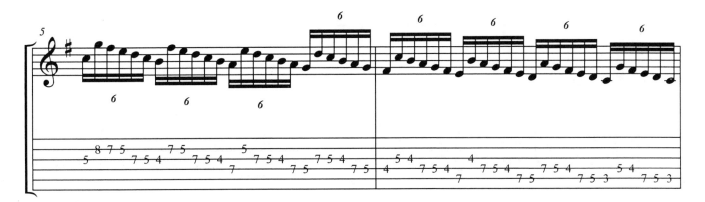

The next two use wide interval skips, radical string crossing, string skipping, and challenging fret hand stretches. **Track 16** moves the interval of a 3rd through the scale in a predictable pattern, while **track 17** uses the wider (and more challenging) 6th interval in a string skipping fiesta. Be sure to alternate pick starting with a down stroke.

Track 16

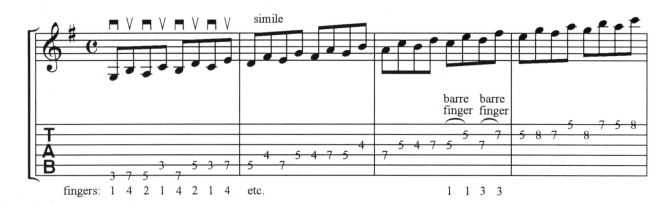

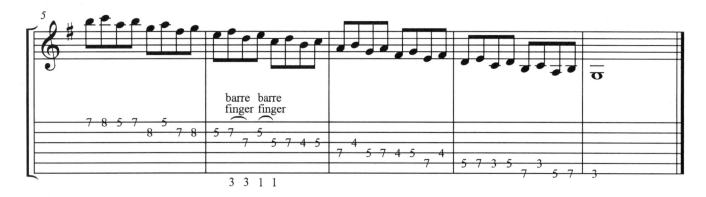

Track 17

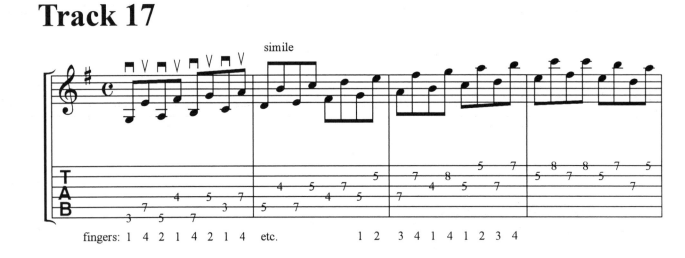

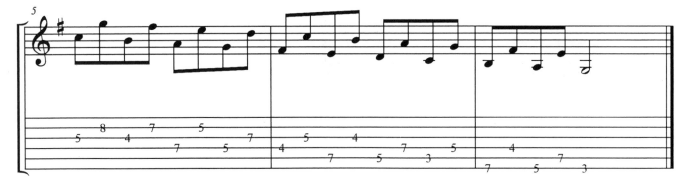

Hammer Ons and Pull Offs

    Leave each finger down on the string as you execute the hammer ons for **track 18**. For the pull offs, all four fingers should be planted on the string, then pull off one at a time. Strive to keep a consistent volume between hammer ons, pull offs, and picked notes. For hammer ons, visualize the finger as a small hammer pounding a nail into the fret board. For pull offs, yank the finger tip from the string in a downwards motion with enough force to pluck the string, rather than simply lifting the finger off the string in a perpendicular motion.

Track 18

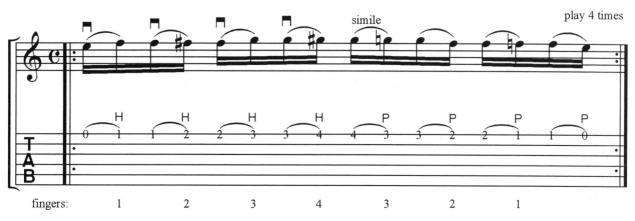

fingers: 1   2   3   4   3   2   1

As you hammer on each three note sequence (**track 19**), leave the fingers planted, so by the third note on each string all three fingers are anchored firmly on the string. Next, release all three fingers and move swiftly to the next string, repeating the same process. For the pull offs, begin with all three fingers planted on the first string, then pull off one at a time. Repeat this on all remaining strings. This technique is particular to legato style playing (covered later in this volume), where the notes are seamlessly connected creating a slick and polished sound.

Track 19

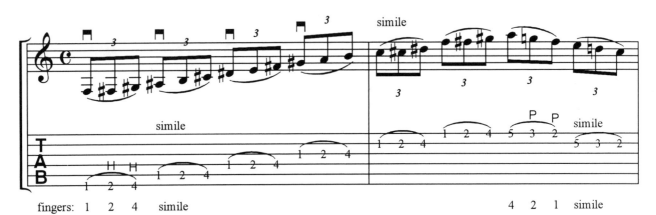

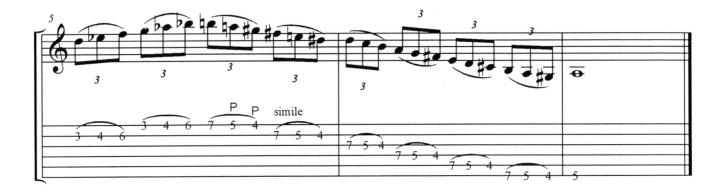

Track 20 uses the same hammer on and pull off technique as the previous, but with fingers one, three, and four.

Track 20

Trills

One of the surest ways to build finger speed, stamina, and strength is with *trills*. A trill is the rapid alternation of two notes usually performed with hammer ons and pull offs. I've designed two exercises that use all four fingers in different combinations. These exercises are especially great for building pinkie strength. Start out slow at first, then gradually build up speed. For **tracks 21 and 22** pick the first note of each trill and let your fingers do the rest. The exact number of notes in the trill can vary and also depends on the performers skill level. A beginner might have only four notes in the trill, while a more advanced player could successfully execute eight or more. Next, repeat the exercise on the remaining strings.

Track 21

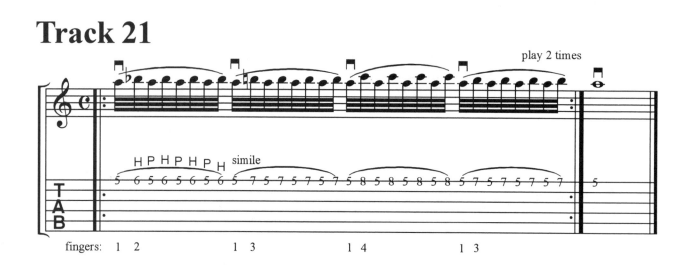

fingers: 1   2   1   3   1   4   1   3

Track 22

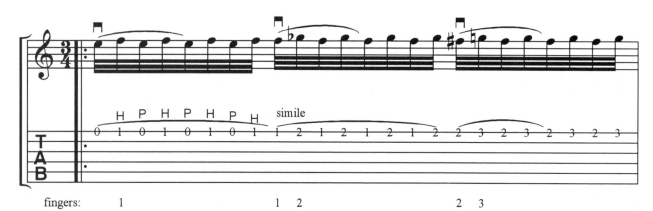

fingers: 1   1   2   2   3

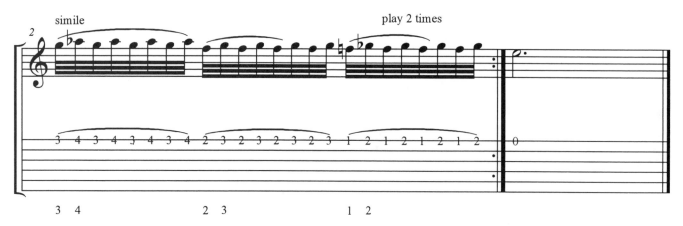

3   4   2   3   1   2

Melodic Exercises

Inspired by AC/DC, **track 23** uses repeating pull offs to the open B string, which acts as the *pedal point*. A pedal point is a note that is held while the other notes move above or below. This technique is common in classical music and specifically in the music of composer J. S. Bach. Make sure the pull offs are played evenly so all four sixteenth notes in the lick are the same distance apart.

Track 23

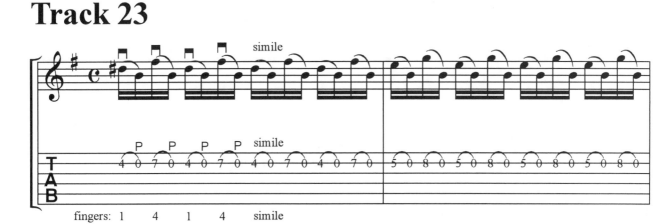

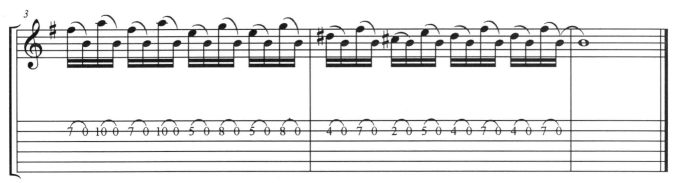

Track 24 and 25 are variations on the previous exercise. These types of exercises are great for building pinkie coordination and strength.

Track 24

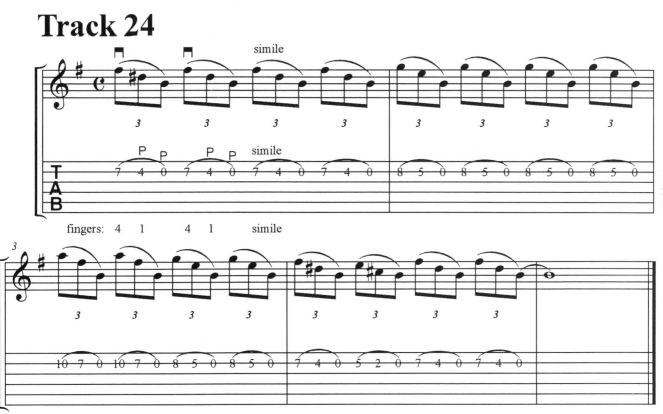

Track 25

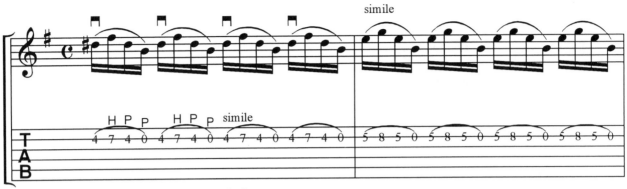

Inside and Outside Picking

With the exception of sweep picking (two or more consecutive down or up strokes) there are only two possible ways to pick when crossing from one string to an adjacent string: either down-up or up-down. Play the two examples below and notice how the same lick feels with *inside* and *outside* picking. For *inside* picking, the pick seems to move back and forth from in between the two strings, while *outside* picking has the pick attacking the two strings from the outer side. Even though most guitarists find outside picking to be the easiest and most comfortable, both should be practiced.

Inside picking   ## Outside picking

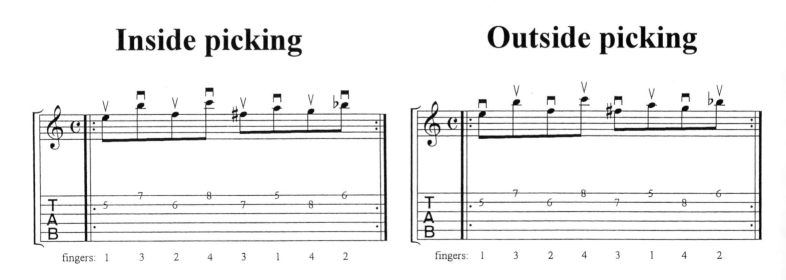

Track 26 is designed to specifically develop outside picking. To work on inside picking, start the example with an up stroke and alternate pick.

Track 26

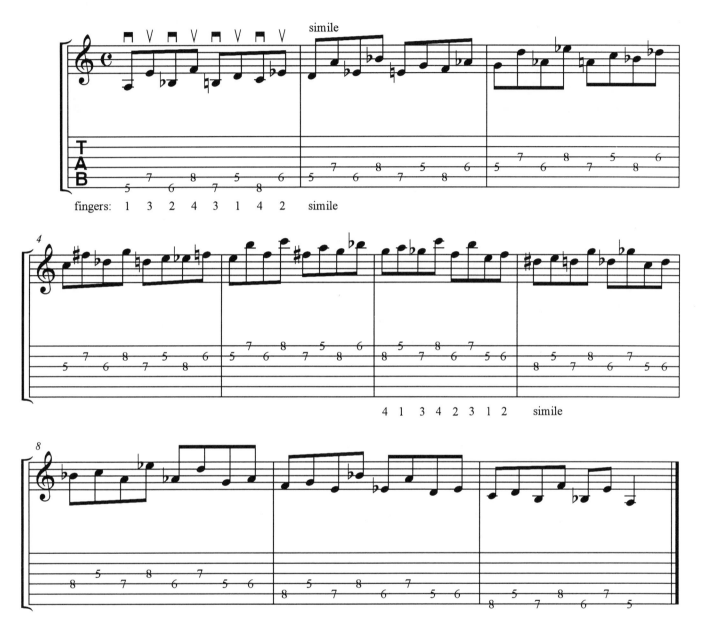

Short Speed Bursts

Have you ever wondered how some guitarists can pick ultra fast flurries of notes that fly by at lightning speed? One way is to workout with a metronome, starting out slowly and gradually increasing tempo as the fingers and pick memorize the passage, only playing as fast as you can with no mistakes. If there is inconsistency with the picking or fingering, then slow down to a comfortable tempo. Another way is to take short little musical passages, called *speed bursts*, and play the line as fast as you can one time, then stop and repeat. The tempo you should shoot for is sextuplets (six notes per beat) at about 110 on the metronome. At each stop analyze what you just played by asking critical questions like "was the pick synchronized with the fingers?" and "did I alternate pick?".

Track 27 illustrates one short speed burst moved diatonically through the scale. Here you'll play the quick burst two times before moving to the next lick. Start out with the metronome set to a slow tempo where you can play the sextuplet evenly on one beat. The last note of the lick is on the second beat.

Track 27

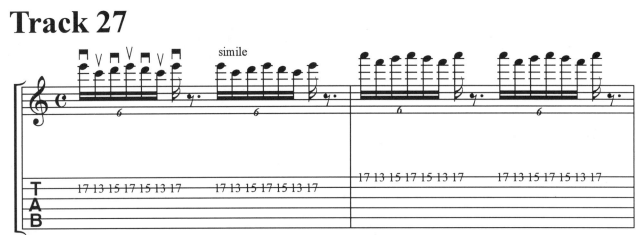

fingers: 4 1 2 4 2 1 4

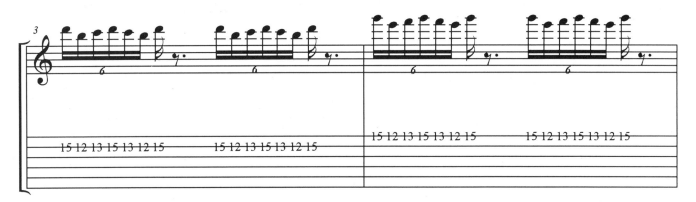

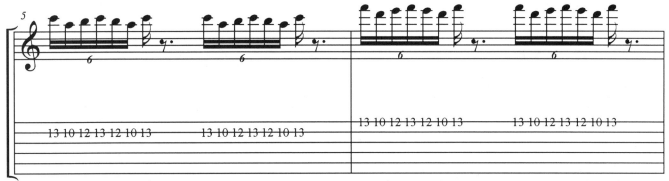

4 1 3 4 3 1 4

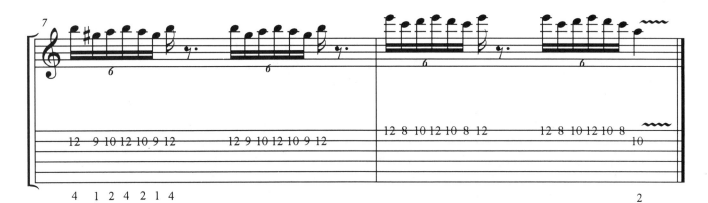

4 1 2 4 2 1 4

2

Once you can perform the short speed bursts effectively, try extending the burst as on **track 28**. Here, the lick repeats three times before resolving on beat four. If you're having trouble performing the lick with any degree of speed, go back to the tremolo exercises earlier in this volume and spend more time on this technique. I've found that having a well developed tremolo technique helps this type of speed picking.

Track 28

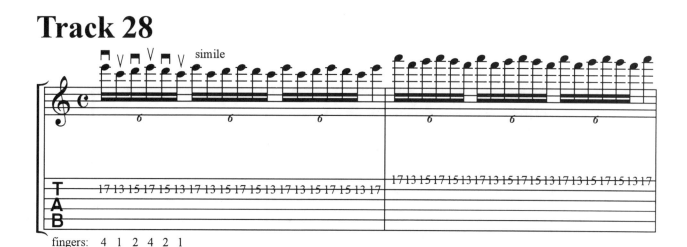

fingers: 4 1 2 4 2 1

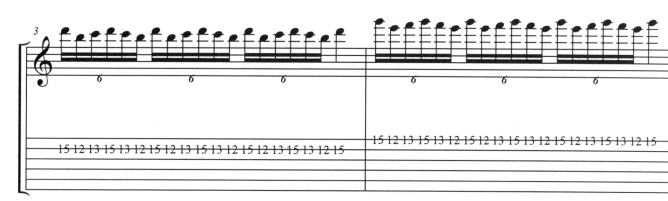

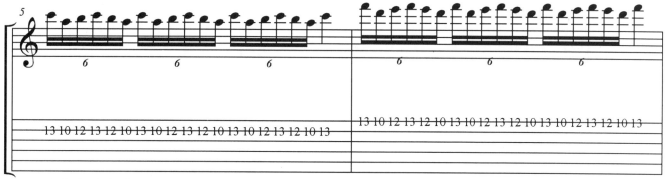

4 1 3 4 3 1

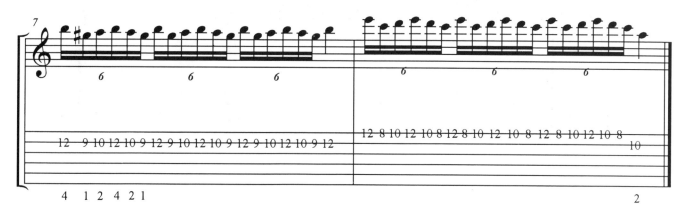

4 1 2 4 2 1

Below are four short exercises to advance the speed bursts. These incorporate one or more notes from an adjacent string. Begin with an up stroke for the first three exercises (**tracks 29, 30, and 31**) and a down stroke for **track 32.** Using these specific picking patterns allows the pick to cross over to the next string with the least amount of effort.

Track 29

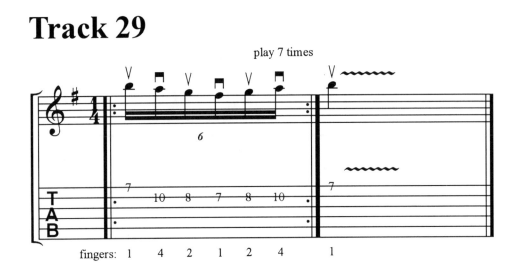

fingers: 1   4   2   1   2   4   1

Track 30

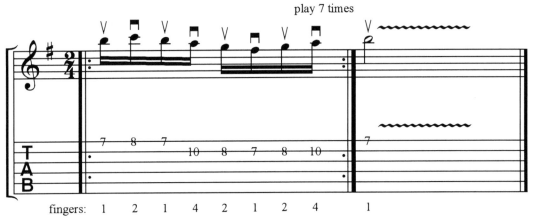

fingers: 1   2   1   4   2   1   2   4   1

Track 31

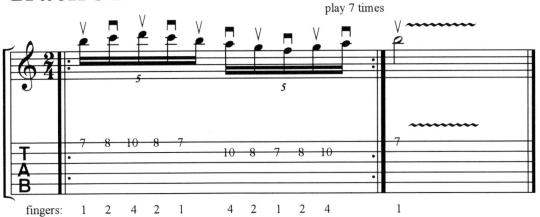

fingers: 1   2   4   2   1   4   2   1   2   4   1

30

Track 32

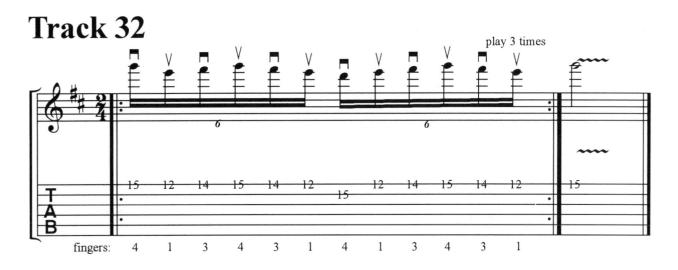

Once the fingers feel comfortable with these short sequences, you're ready to move across the fret board. **Track 33** moves the previous exercise (track 32) across the strings in a descending manner through the E dorian scale.

Track 33

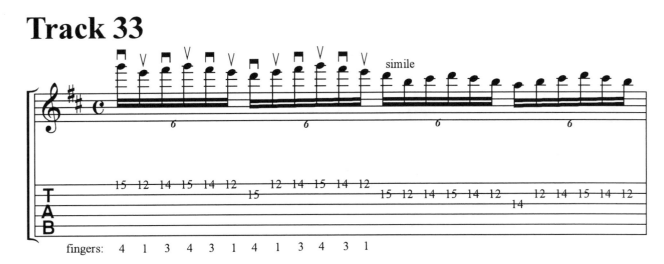

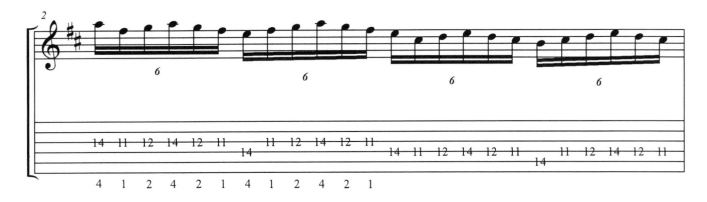

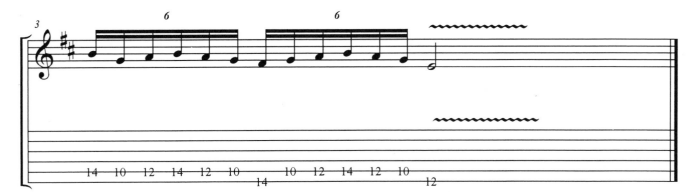

Here's an Al Di Meola inspired sequence lick that ascends through the E dorian scale (**track 34**).

Track 34

fingers: 1 2 4 1 2 4

1 2 4 1 4 2

1 3 4   1 3 4 4 2 1

4 2 1 2 4 1 2 4 4

32

Sweep Picking

One of the supreme rages for 80's 'metal and shred' guitarists was sweep picking. The slick sonority, which is achieved by using the same pick stroke when crossing two or more adjacent strings in succession, was an integral part of the genres lexicon. This economical picking form is most commonly used to execute arpeggios, and guitarists Frank Gambale, Yngwie Malmsteen, and Paul Gilbert are credited with popularizing the technique. Strive to keep each note separate by fretting one note at a time and don't let the notes bleed into each other. Most guitarists attempting the sweep for the first time find it awkward, so I've designed two exercises to help develop the technique. **Track 35** works on the down strokes with a series of short speed bursts, while **track 36** isolates the up strokes in the same manner. Think of the pick as making one big down or up stroke that crosses all four strings rather than four separate pick strokes. After the pick strikes the string it should immediately come to rest on the next string, ready to strike (similar to the rest stroke in classical guitar). Fret only one finger at a time so the notes don't ring out over each other.

Track 35

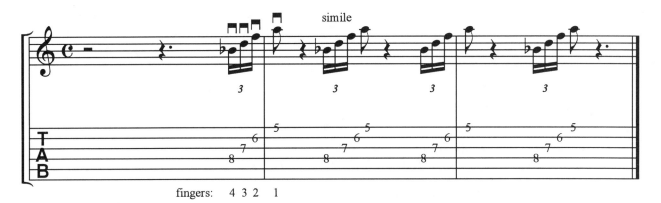

Track 36

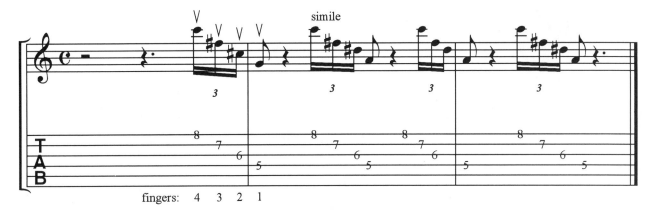

Track 37 combines the two previous exercises to make an 'X' shape on the fret board. Endeavor to attain a smooth and even sound in both directions.

Track 37

fingers:　4　3　2　1　4　3　2　1　simile

Vibrato

Having a smooth and controlled vibrato is as important as alternate picking, and it's the one element that separates the amateurs from the pros. No matter how fast or technical you can play, a weak or uncontrolled vibrato will place you in the lower ranks of the guitar community. Listen to the distinct vibratos of B.B. King, Ace Frehley, Edward Van Halen, and Yngwie Malmsteen for instance. There's are controlled and soothing, while a lesser guitarist's sounds uneven, nervous, and inconsistent. Since no two guitarists have the same vibrato, it makes sense to develop yours, for this is one of the trademarks that will define your style.

Vibrato produces a shivering sonority that is added to most sustained notes by quickly and repeatedly bending the string up and down (with a rocking motion). This is usually done in time with the song and the bends should be a consistent quarter, half, or whole step. The concept sounds simple, but mastering the technique might prove challenging. Below is an example illustrating vibrato. Example 1 shows vibrato added to a note in standard notation, while example 2 breaks it down to show the individual bending motions.

Examples of vibrato

example 1   example 2

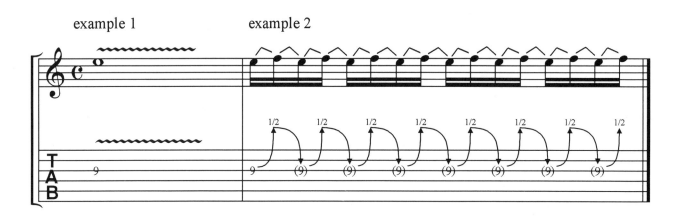

Use the third finger to fret the vibrato in the example above, while the second finger reinforces on the same string by butting up against the third (similar to the string bending technique of using two or more fingers to bend). To ensure a good grip wrap the fretting hand thumb over the top edge of the guitar neck. The rhythm of the vibrato should be even and the bending pitch should be consistent. An erratic and inconsistent vibrato is unpleasant to listen to and should be avoided. After getting the hang of vibrato with the third finger, take a crack at it with the remaining fingers. Ultimately, all the fingers should be able comfortable with the technique.

Use vibrato on every note from **track 38** and watch the fingering. Notice throughout the exercise all four fingers are used.

Track 38

String Bending

In the world of string bending, the whole step and half step bends are the most common. These are the two smallest intervals in the standard twelve tone chromatic scale. A 'half step' is the equivalent of any two notes on one string that are one fret apart, while a 'whole step' is two frets apart. There should always be a target note the bend is aiming for and it's usually another scale tone. Your ear needs to 'hear' the note it's bending to and the fingers will push the string up to match. Try this test: first, play the 9th fret on the 'G' string and let your ear memorize this pitch. Next, play the 7th fret on the same string and bend it up (towards the ceiling) to match the previous pitch.

35

The most common fingers used for string bending are the strong second (middle), and third (ring), although the first and fourth are not immune to bends. For bends with the third finger, reinforcement is added by aligning the second finger (and first if necessary) on the same string, butting it up to the third, creating one big 'fat' finger. A second finger bend is supported with the first finger, while the rare fourth finger bend is backed up by the second and third. The lonely first finger is left to muster up all it's strength to bend strings by itself. Ouch!! Generally, bending on the top three strings (G, B, and E) involves 'pushing' the string up towards the ceiling, while bending on the three bass strings (E, A, and D) is a 'pulling' motion towards the floor. Additional leverage comes from wrapping the fretting hand thumb over the top edge of the guitar neck (check out B.B. King or Stevie Ray Vaughan any time they bend strings).

The bending action is a rotating motion from the wrist rather than moving the fingers. The fingers are held rigidly in a locked position while the hand pivots from the point of contact where the index finger connects to the hand and the bottom edge of the guitar neck.

Track 39 is an exercise that let's you hear the note you'll bend to first (the third note in every two beat phrase is the 'target note'), then proceed to bend the next note up to match what you've just heard. Let your ear guide the fingers to the correct pitch. Proper intonation is requisite, otherwise the bend will sound out of tune.

Track 39

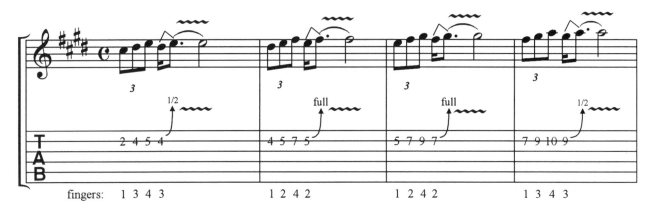

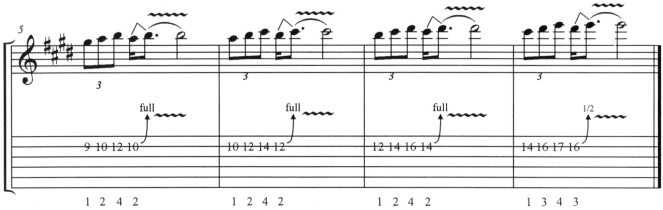

Here's an exercise using *prebends* (**track 40**). Before picking, prebend the string to the desired pitch, then pick the bent note and release the string to it's normal unbent position. Since your ear doesn't have a reference note to hear first, the fingers must 'feel' what a half and whole step bend are like.

Track 40

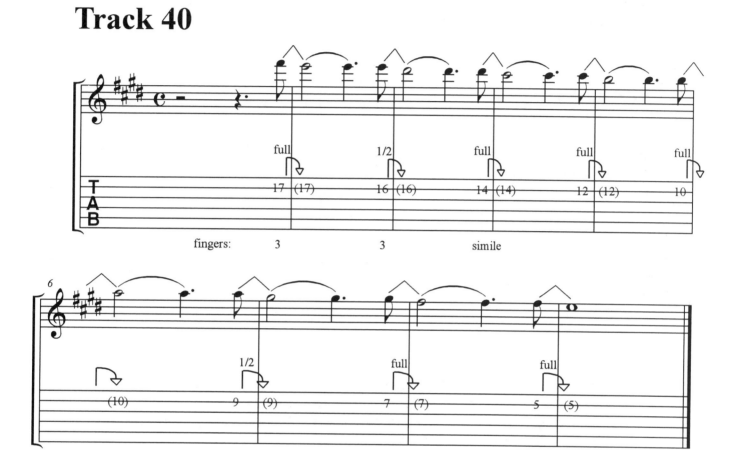

Track 41 works it's way up the second string with a popular bending lick in D major. Each lick begins with a whole or half step bend to the next scale degree, followed by a release of the bend and a pull off. Continue moving this sequence up the neck diatonically (keeping all the notes in the same key). Try this exercise in G major by moving to the first string and playing the same fret positions. By the way, if you're getting unwanted string noise from the neighboring lower strings when bending, try resting the picking hand palm on the bass strings (like the palm muting technique).

Track 41

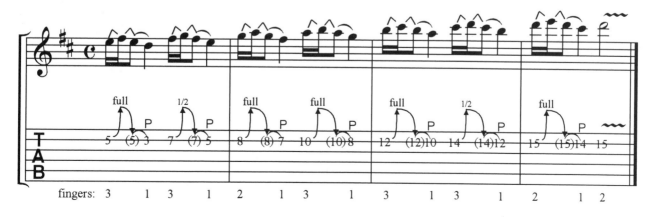

A *unison bend* occurs when two different notes on adjacent strings are played at the same time and the lower of the two notes is bent up to match the higher. Your ear will guide your fingers to the correct pitch. On **track 42** use the first finger for the notes on the second string, while the third finger (supported by the second finger) handles the bends on the third string. Listen for proper intonation by stopping the bending motion once your ear hears both notes match. Be careful to bend far enough and not too far, as this will sound out of tune.

Track 42

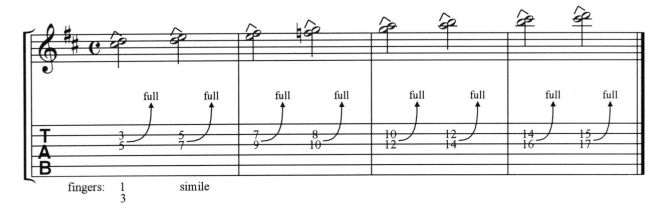

For a cool effect try adding vibrato to the bent note (**track 43**). This subtle pitch variation will cover slight intonation errors, especially when playing with distortion. Many guitarists including Jimi Hendrix, Ace Frehley, Steve Vai, and Edward Van Halen use unison bends quite effectively to create melodies.

Track 43

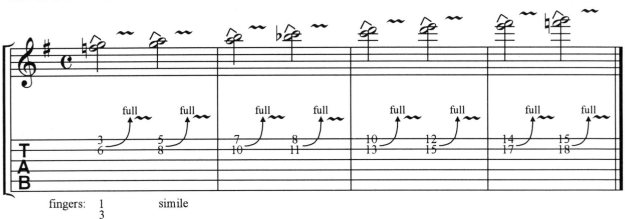

In the field of blues a subtle yet powerful tool is the *micro-tone bend*, which is actually a quarter step bend (**track 44**). The target note is the 'true blues note' between the major and minor 3rd, and major and minor 7th. To hear this, play the eleventh fret on the first string (minor 3rd of 'C'), then play the twelfth fret (major 3rd of 'C') on the same string. Next, bend the eleventh fret up slightly, just shy of the twelfth fret pitch that you just heard. These slightly out of tune pitches create tension which is resolved at the next note. This battle between tension and resolution is a corner stone in many forms of music including blues, jazz, rock, and metal. Mike Bloomfield's cutting electric blues features quite a bit of micro-tonal bending. Check out his playing on Electric Flags "Goin' Down Slow" and "Texas".

Track 44

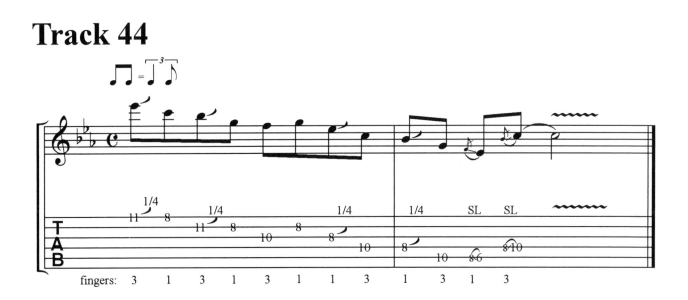

Now for some mighty string bending with attitude. These short repeating phrases (**tracks 45, 46, 47, 48, 49, 50, and 51**) are part of the rock, metal, and blues lexicon and must be learned. These licks should be rehearsed until they can be performed as freely as words flowing in a conversation. The pick indications are marked above the music.

Track 45

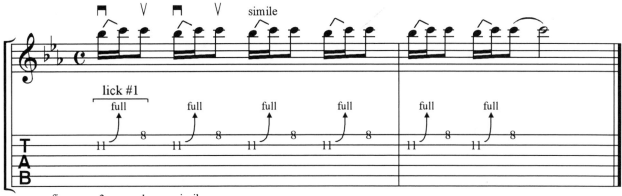

Track 46

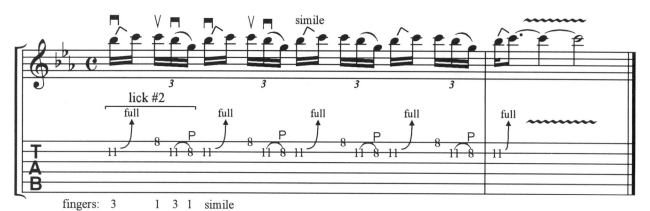

fingers: 3   1 3 1 simile

Track 47

fingers: 3   1 1 4 1 simile

Track 48

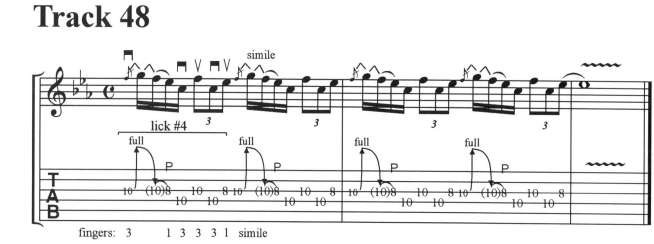

fingers: 3   1 3 3 3 1 simile

Track 49

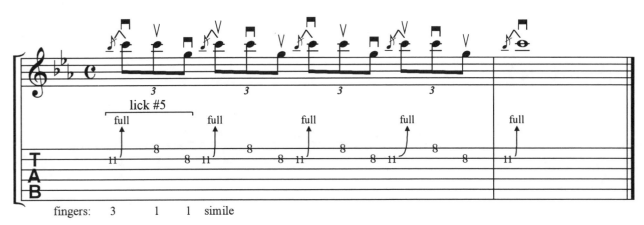

Track 50

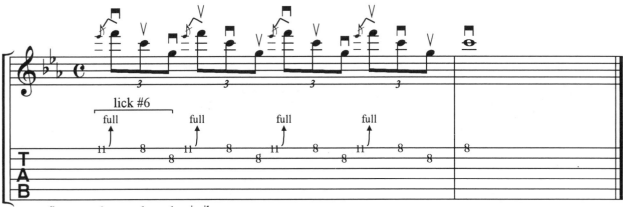

Track 51

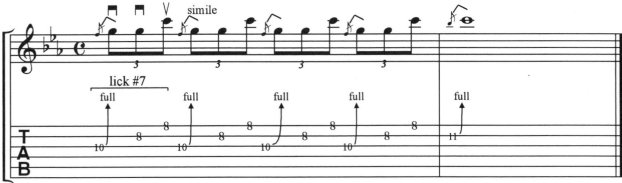

Most solos can be broken down to reveal separate melodic ideas (licks) strung together to create the illusion of one long musical statement. Think of the separate licks as words that make up a sentence. Rearrange the words and it says something else. **Track 52** is a short solo comprising most of the licks from the previous seven tracks.

Track 52

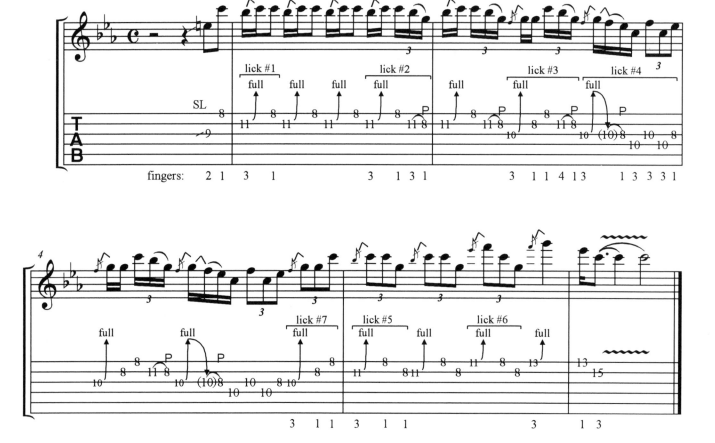

Legato

A favored technique among shred style guitarists is *legato*, which means to play smoothly and in a connected manner, without any breaks between the notes. The idea is to pick as few notes as possible while generating sound with hammer ons, pull offs, slides, and tapping. Since this style doesn't require many pick attacks the potential for ultra fast, fluid, and clean melodic lines is unbridled. If every note was picked then much time would need to be spent on synchronizing the picking with the fretting fingers, and one of the most common reasons for sloppy guitar playing is when the picking are not locked in with the fingers, therefore you may find it easier to execute fleet fingered lines using legato technique. Note: if your picking is a little sloppy you should be concentrating on exercises that require you to pick every note to build coordination between the two hands, rather than avoiding the area.

This first legato exercise (**track 53**) meanders it's way up through the A minor scale using hammer ons and pull offs. Notice that the first note of each string is always picked.

Track 53

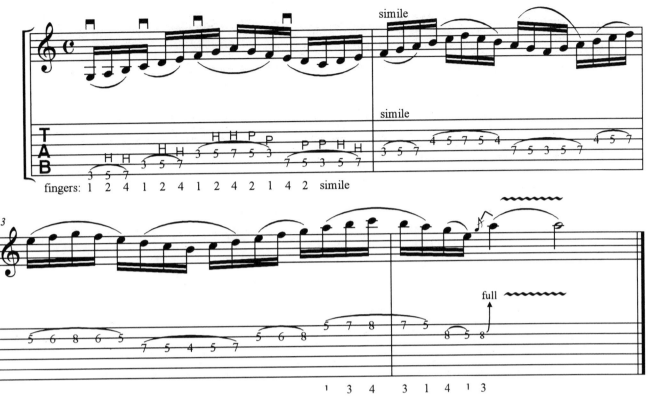

Here's an idea inspired by Joe Satriani's legato playing (**track 54**) that descends through A minor using pull offs, slides, and hammer ons. Pick the first of every eight notes and let the fretting fingers do the rest. The last seven notes are played in 'three notes per string' fashion. Strive to make all notes the same volume, whether performed with a pick, pull off, etc. Try learning and mastering one string at a time, then put it all together.

Track 54

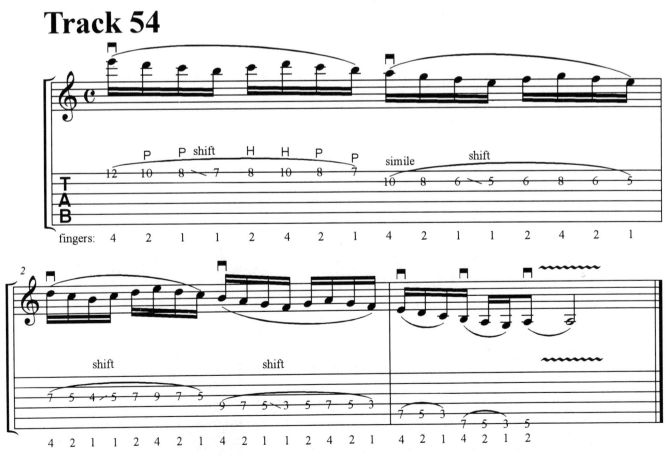

43

Combining scales can create interesting melodies and new scale shapes. **Track 55** is a composite dorian/blues scale in the key of A. Notice the pattern uses three notes per string and the fingering on each string is first, second, and fourth. Watch for the 'two string' sweep picking motion (two down strokes) that occurs five times throughout the run. Break down the run by learning the first seven notes, then proceed to the next seven, and so on.

Track 55

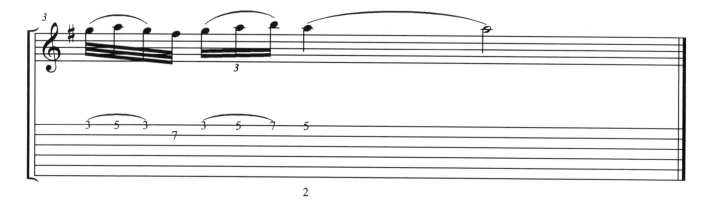

This slick legato run (**track 56**) is embodied with the usual assortment of techniques, and is one heck of a left hand work out. Try to keep all the notes evenly spaced, and work on one string at a time.

Track 56

Here's an exotic sounding run (**track 57**) that descends through E phrygian.
Notice the quintuplet (groupings of five notes per beat) on the fourth beat of bars 1
and 2 that produces a slightly 'rushed' feeling.

Track 57

This next legato exercise (**track 58**) is a short solo that ascends through the E aeolian scale (with the exception of the 'flat 5' blues notes in bar 3), then in the last three bars (7-9) modulates to E dorian. I felt this sounded better played freely, so there is no metronome click track. Use the rhythms in the notation as a general guide. Endeavor to connect all the separate licks evenly so the piece flows.

Track 58

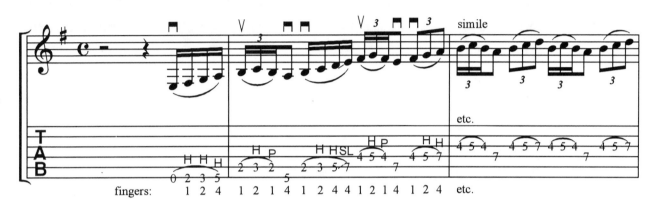

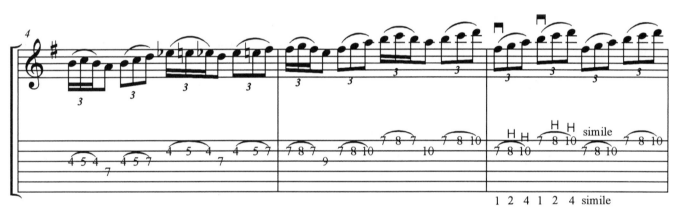

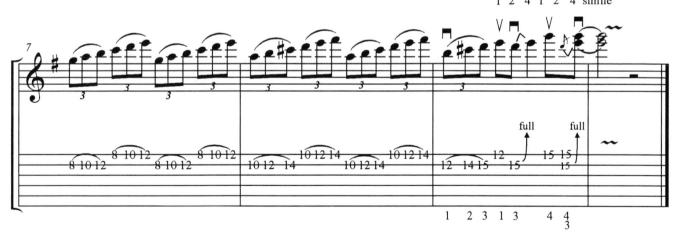

47

The last two legato exercises incorporate tapping to produce silky slick phrases. Most guitarists use the picking hand index finger to execute the tap, while cupping the pick in the palm of the same hand. **Track 59** is based on a familiar six note sequence that most guitarists usually pick. Here, the tapping technique proves to be a crucial element in making this lick sparkle as it slithers down the high E string, and then finally descending across the remaining strings.

Track 59

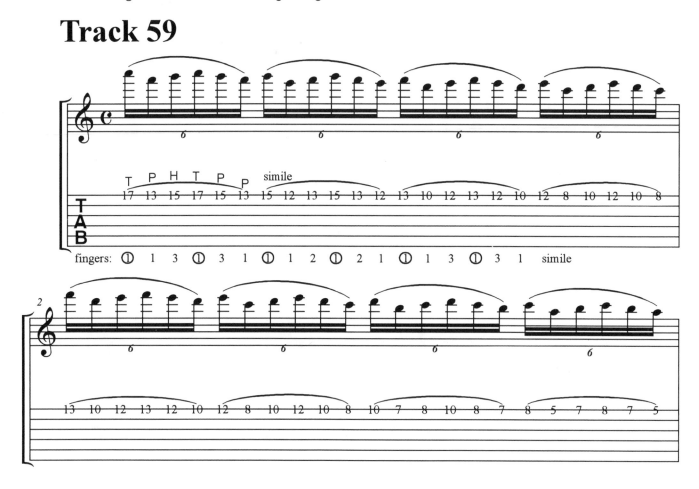

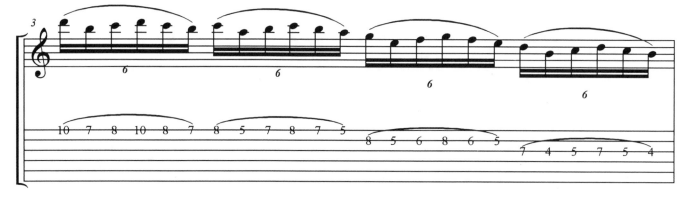

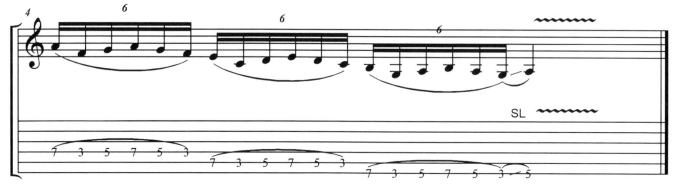

The second tapping idea (**track 60**) is based on a sequence of fours that meanders it's way across the strings and up the fret board to resolve on G. Both runs (tracks 59 and 69) should be played as smooth and even as possible, with no gaps or stuttering.

Track 60

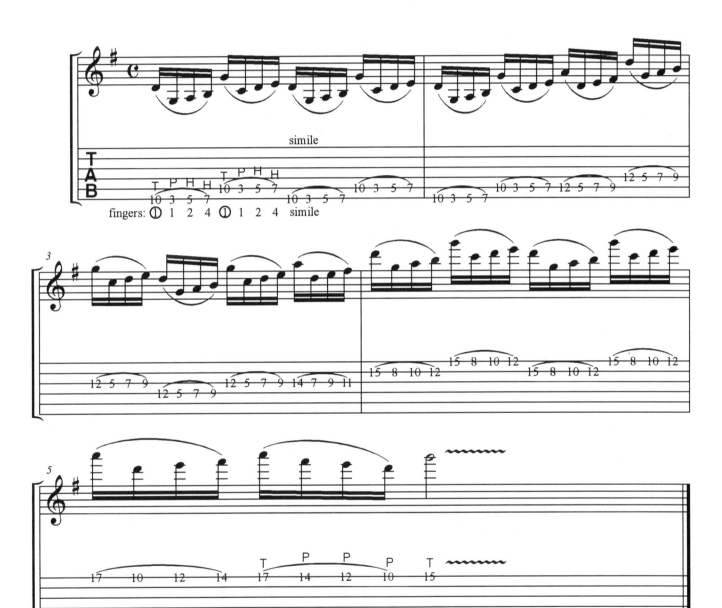

Arpeggios

Edward Van Halen taps them with fury, Frank Gambale and Yngwie Malmsteen sweep pick effortlessly across the fret board with them, and Paul Gilbert and Eric Johnson use string skipping techniques to perform these intervallic shapes. Give up? They're called *arpeggios*.

An arpeggio is the notes of a chord played individually as opposed to all at once, like when strumming a chord. A common and very useful form of arpeggio is the *triad* (three note chord), which is the fundamental building block for major, minor, and diminished chords. The three notes are identified as the root, 3rd, and 5th (1-3-5). These numbers represent scale degrees from the scale chord is derived from. Take the D major scale (D-E-F#-G-A-B-C#-D) for example, and assign a number to each note in sequential order (D=1, E=2, F#=3, G=4, A=5, B=6, C#=7, and D=1 or 8-octave). Play the 1st, 3rd, and 5th notes (D-F#-A) individually and you've got a D major triad played arpeggio style. Think of an arpeggio as taking every other note from the scale. For 7th chord arpeggios (D maj.7) simply add the 7th (C#) to the triad = D-F#-A-C#.

This system for finding chords and arpeggios can be applied to all the other notes in D major as well. For instance, the second chord in D major is built from the second note (E), and by adding every other note from E you arrive at E-G-B. This makes an E minor triad. **Track 61** demonstrates this procedure for all the triads inherent to the key of D major on the first and second strings. Realize that the notes of these arpeggios can be played in any order and some of the more interesting sounding arpeggio style licks are often ones that displace the order of the three notes. More on this later.

Track 61

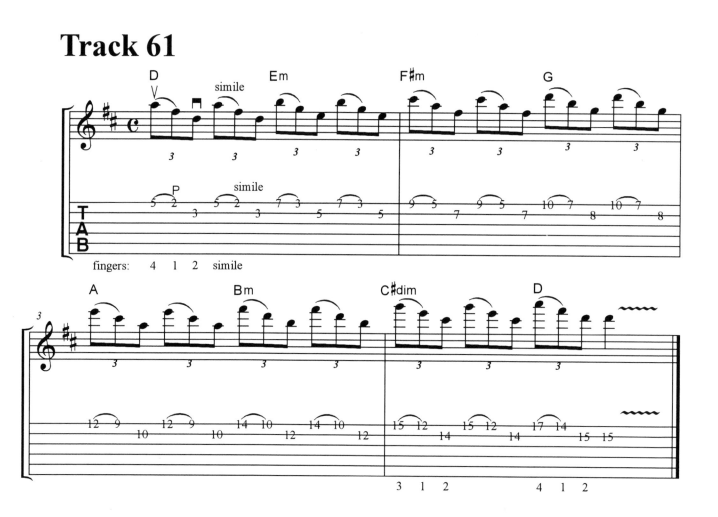

50

There are three fundamental triad chord qualities stemming from the major scale- major (1-3-5), minor (1-♭3-5), and diminished (1,♭3,♭5). The distance between each chord tone determines it's quality (major, minor, or diminished).

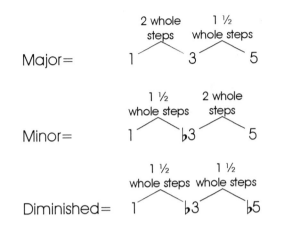

Major=

2 whole steps   1 ½ whole steps

1   3   5

Minor=

1 ½ whole steps   2 whole steps

1   ♭3   5

Diminished=

1 ½ whole steps   1 ½ whole steps

1   ♭3   ♭5

In music lingo the terms 'half step' and 'whole step' refer to the smallest and next to smallest intervals in the chromatic scale. A half step equals the distance between two notes that are one fret apart on the same string (F# to G or C# to D etc.), while a whole step is two notes apart on the same string (G to A or D to E etc.).

Track 62 extends the triad shapes in D major to cover three strings. To execute this effectively try sweep picking three down strokes followed by two up strokes, with a pull off between the two ups.

Track 62

Once the triadic arpeggio shapes are learned, the next logical step is to add the 7th scale degree to each chord. For instance, to find the 7th of a C major chord, count up *seven* scale degrees from the root note 'C' (include C as the first in the series). Hint, there are no sharps or flats in the key of C, therefore the 7th note up from C is 'B'. Add this note to the already existing C major triad (C-E-G) and you've got 'C major 7' (C-E-G-B). **Track 63** shows one way this could be applied to the chords in C major using sweep picking. First, learn the individual arpeggio shapes by playing each four consecutive times without stopping, then connect the entire series playing each one time.

Track 63

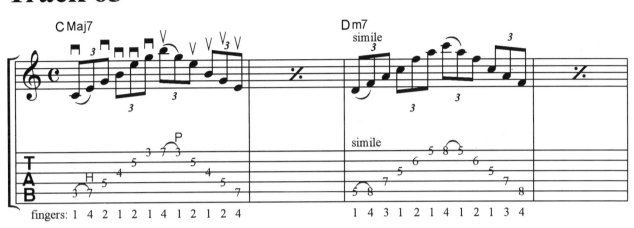

fingers: 1 4 2 1 2 1 4 1 2 1 2 4   1 4 3 1 2 1 4 1 2 1 3 4

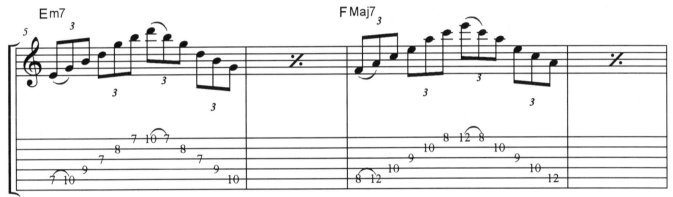

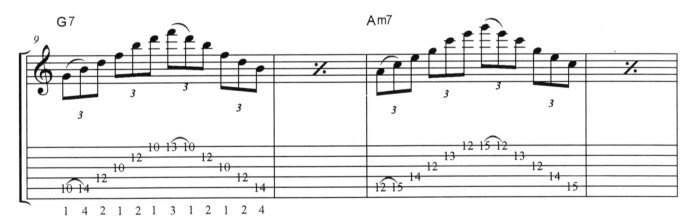

1 4 2 1 2 1 3 1 2 1 2 4

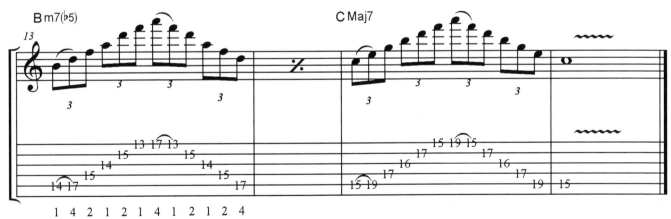

1 4 2 1 2 1 4 1 2 1 2 4

Try mixing up the notes of the arpeggios by arranging the notes in less predictable patterns. **Track 64** takes a standard three string shape and turns it into a shred fest of small sweep picking motions.

Track 64

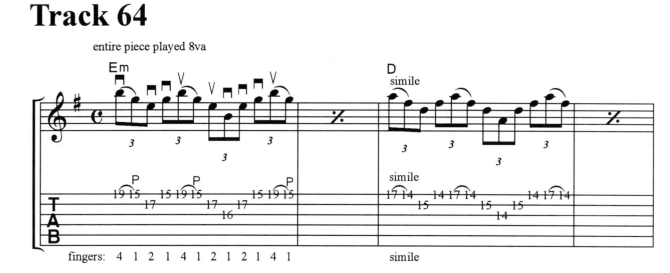

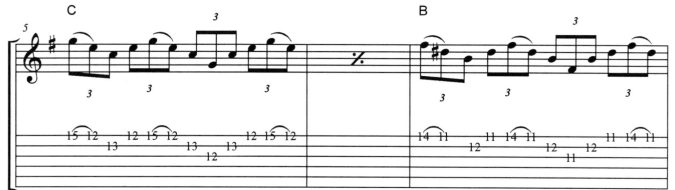

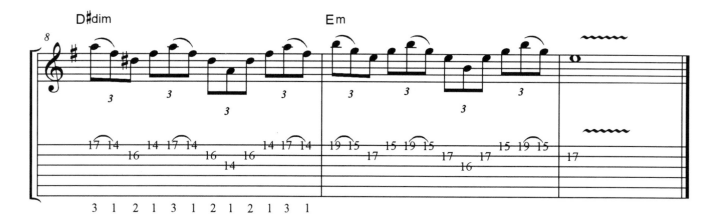

The next exercise (**track 65**) arranges the arpeggio notes in a classically inspired sequence. Here, the notes 'skip' from root to 5th, flat 3rd to root, and 5th to flat 3rd. Although the sequence is grouped in 'twos', the rhythm is played with a triplet feel creating a less predictable pattern. The 'outside' picking used for this etude makes it quite comfortable to perform. Feel and memorize the dance that the pick and fingers make while crossing the strings.

Track 65

Here's a great 'string skipping' workout with arpeggios over a typical rock chord progression in E minor. Guitarist Paul Gilbert helped popularize string skipping with arpeggio sequences similar to **track 66**. Pay close attention to the pick directions and notice that two consecutive down or up strokes are always sandwiching a pull off or hammer on in between. Essentially, alternate picking is used and a pull off or hammer on takes the place of the pick stroke that would have been used. This makes the lick more comfortable to play at lightning speeds.

Track 66

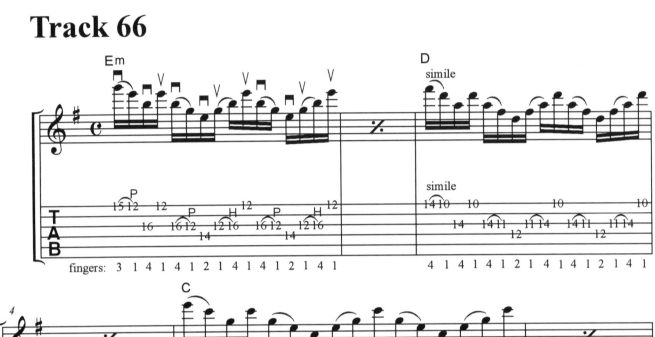

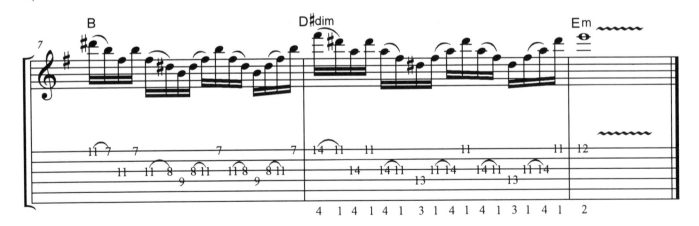

On **track 67** the speedy little lick is based on the two string triad shapes discussed earlier, with the exception of an additional '4th' degree. Use the same picking technique as the previous track, where the pull off takes the place of the up stroke. Again, the triads follow a familiar chord progression, this time in A minor.

Track 67

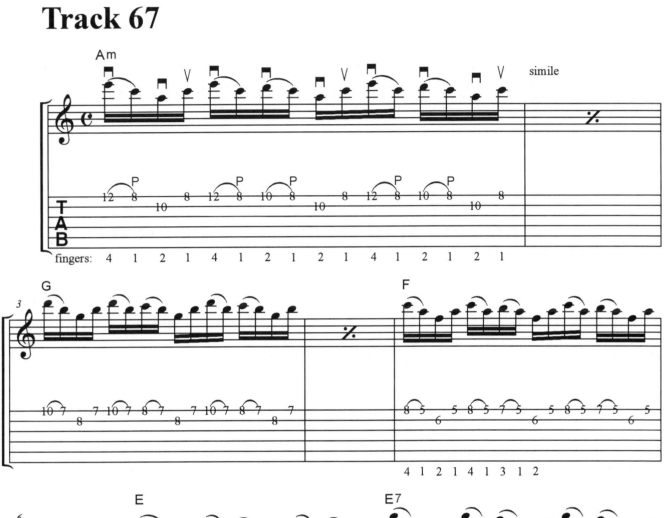

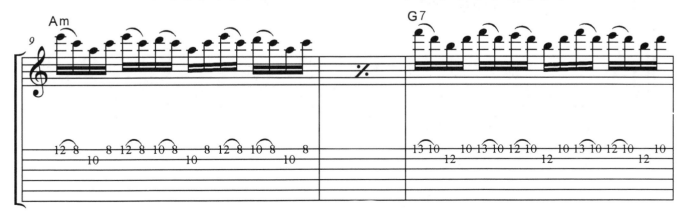

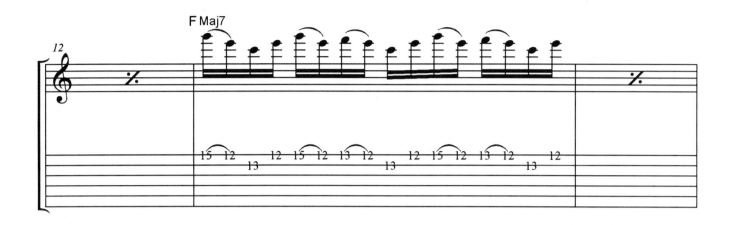

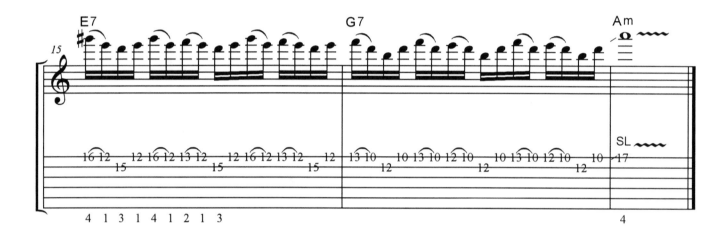

For this Steve Vai inspired idea (**track 68**) I've combined two identical shapes that occur on different sets of strings. The shapes individually make 7th and 6th chords, and when combined make the colorful 13th chord. Use sweep picking along with an occasional hammer on and pull off.

Track 68

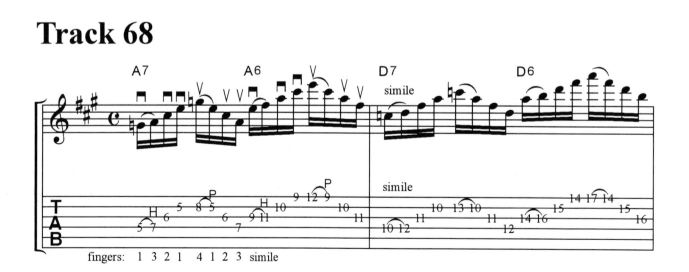

58

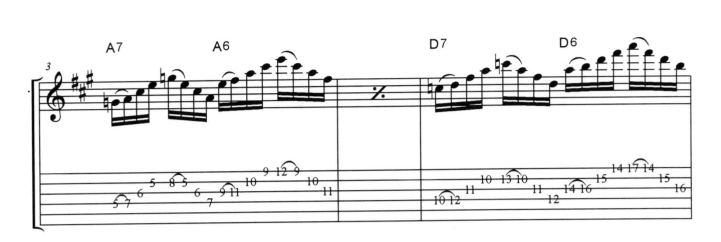

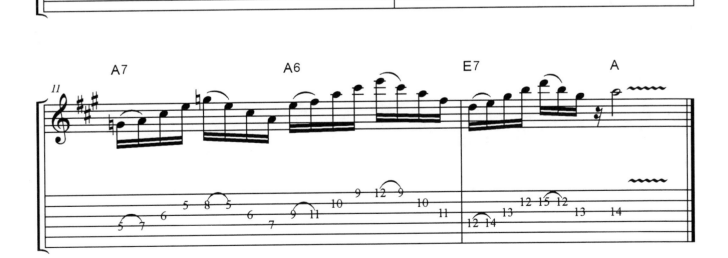

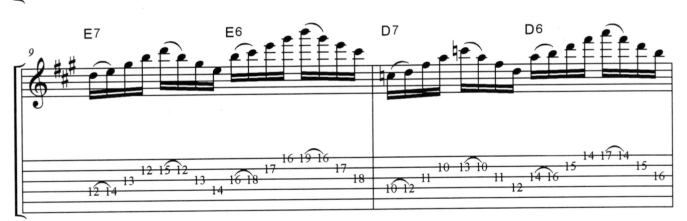

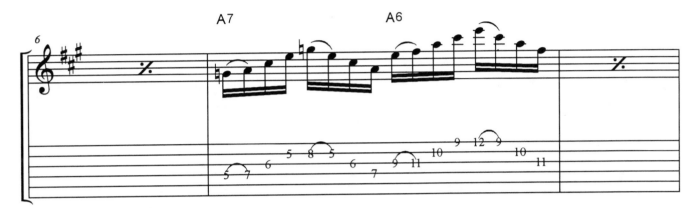

Another popular tool for contemporary guitarists is *two hand tapping*. When used in conjunction with arpeggios, ultra fast and slick lines emerge that are unheard of with conventional picking techniques. You won't need a pick for this technique, so ditch it or cup it in the palm of the picking hand. Support the tapping hand by anchoring the tapping hand thumb on the top edge of the guitar neck above the low E string. Notice that the tapping finger always begins the phrase.

The next two exercises are based on tapping sequences that Edward Van Halen and Randy Rhoads popularized. **Track 69** repeats a triplet sequence (threes) four times before switching to the next chord. All this follows a typical classical progression in A minor that descends through the circle of 5ths.

Track 69

entire piece played 8va

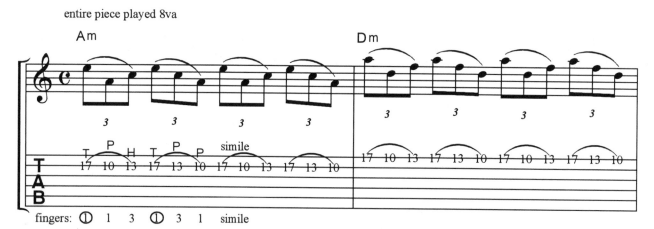

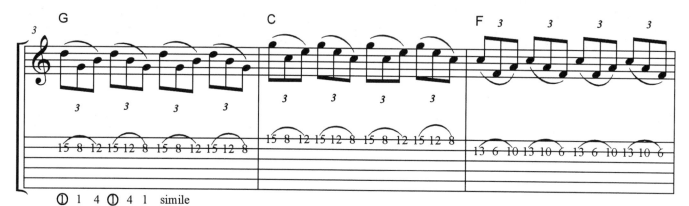

Track 70 is a variation on the previous exercise. Here, the sequence of fours is also repeated four times before moving to the following chord. Play over the same classical chord progression in A minor.

Track 70

entire piece played 8va

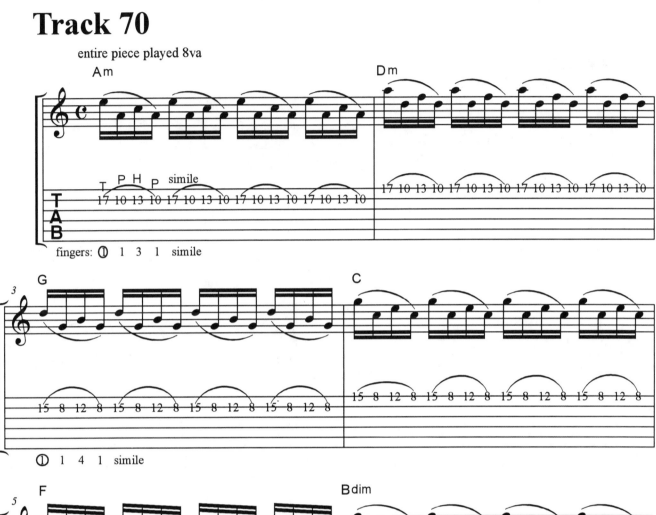

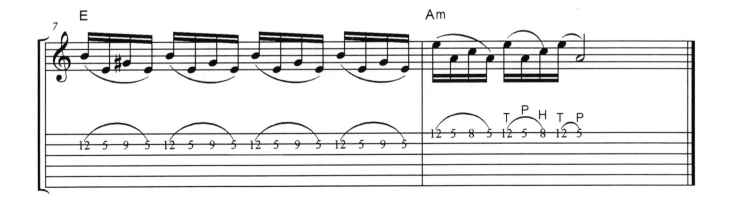

Another essential tapping technique is the Bach inspired *pedal point* method.
This involves consistently tapping the same high note, then pulling off to lower chord
and scale tones on the same string. The idea is to outline enough notes from the chord
to allow your ear to 'hear' the implied chord. **Track 71** demonstrates this, and again,
the sequence is played over the classical progression in A minor.

Track 71

entire piece played 8va

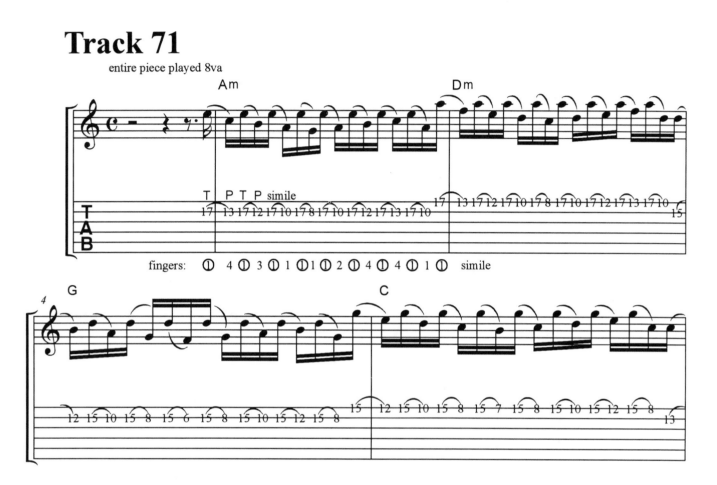

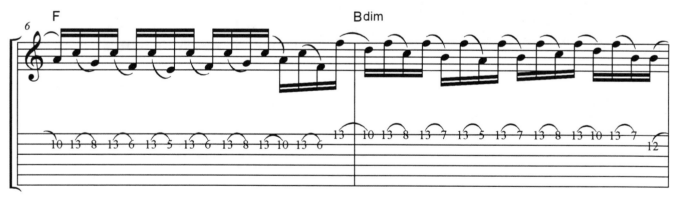

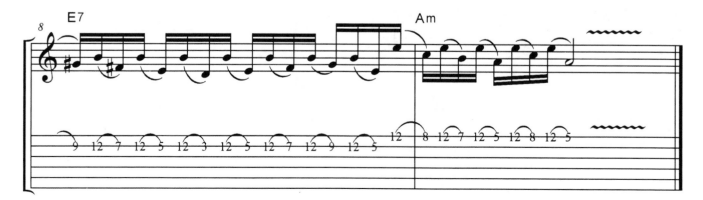

62

For the hard core tapping enthusiasts, the final tapping exercise (**track 72**) incorporates multiple fingers. Use the index, middle, and pinkie fingers to tap this extravaganza. Be sure to support the tapping hand by anchoring the thumb on the top edge of the guitar neck. The tapping fingers should strike the string in a perpendicular manner to gain the most volume and tone. Take this exercise slow and don't let notes ring when changing strings. As you finish playing notes on the second string, release left hand finger pressure just enough to stop the note (*do not* take left hand finger completely off string), then proceed to the next string and repeat this muting technique for the last note on every string.

Track 72

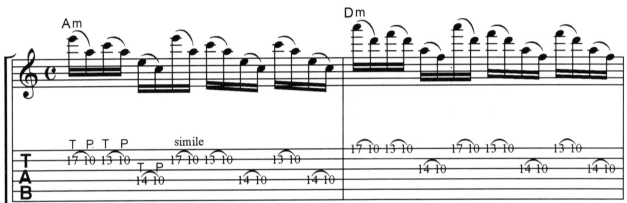

fingers: ④ 3 ② 3 ① 2

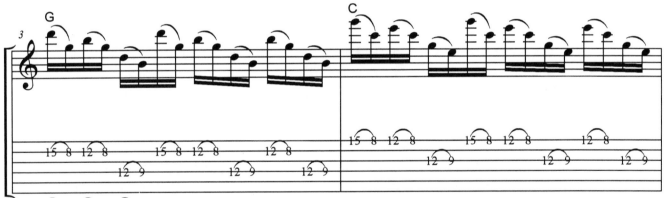

④ 1 ② 1 ① 2

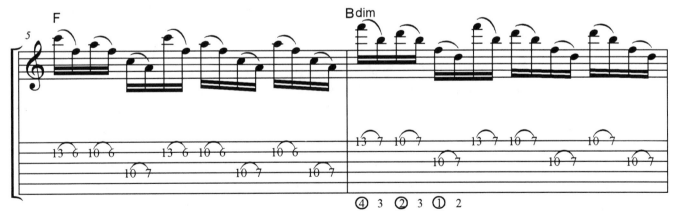

④ 3 ② 3 ① 2

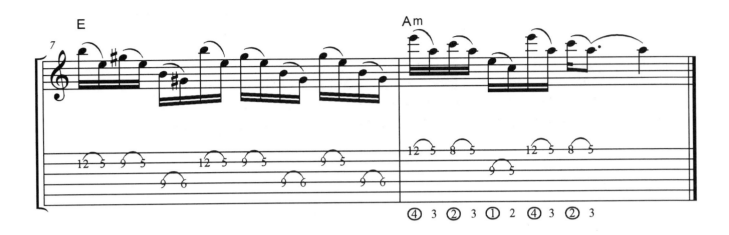

"WORLD MUSIC JAM" LESSON

'World Music Jam' is a song I wrote and included on the accompanying audio CD (**track 73**) to demonstrate a few possible ways of applying the techniques covered in this book. The audio CD also includes a jam along version (with no lead guitar) immediately following the song (**track 74**). Complete transcriptions of the rhythm and lead guitar parts are written below, with the rhythm parts notated first and the lead parts afterwards.

The song is broken down in two distinct sections- 'chorus melody' and 'solos', and both parts are performed over the same chord changes. The chorus melody is always followed by two solo sections and this repeats for most of the song, except for the mellow bridge section.

The tune starts with the chorus, which is a melody derived from the A minor pentatonic scale (see lead guitar solos transcription bars 5-16). Notice the last four bars leave the minor pentatonic scale and gradually meander down the first and second strings following the chords with chord tones. The first solo (bars 17-28) begins with bluesy call and respond ideas, leaving plenty of space between each phrase, and crescendos with a sixteenth note run that follows the descending chords arpeggio style. Excitement builds even more at the second solo (bars 29-40) with a position shift up to the 17th fret and several calculated string bends (bars 29-32). Bars 33-36 return to the 5th fret position for more bluesy string bending riffs in A minor pentatonic. The solo finishes with ascending unison bends juxtaposed against the descending chord progression at bars 37-40 for a counter point idea that rubs nicely with the chords. Adding vibrato to the unison bends brings back memories of the 80's metal guitar style.

The third solo (bars 53-64) adds tension with insane string bending beginning with a half step bend and continuing half step increases up to a few whopping two and one half step bends (bars 53-55). Ouch! Next, a series of bluesy phrases and repetitive string bends work their way towards the unison bends (bars 61-64) which harmonize with the descending chord progression.

At the fourth solo (bars 65-76) I stomped on my phase shifter (MXR Phase 90) set to the slowest sweep. This is the same effect Edward Van Halen used for his solos on the first few Van Halen albums. Here, the solo starts out slow and gradually works up to the speedy quintuplets (five notes per beat). Several of the sections are inspired by exercises from this book, so see if you can spot them. For the run to flow with greatest ease, be sure to use strict alternate picking beginning with a down stroke and the pick should cross the strings using 'outside' picking. The idea hovers around the 7th fret position briefly before descending slightly and then quickly ascending on the first and second strings to climax with a high 'A' bend on the first string. The solo concludes with an incredibly fast 32nd note tapping run on the second string (bars 73-75). Here's the secret for playing this tapping lick fast: the note tapped with the picking hand is also hammered on by the fretting hand, and both are followed by a pull off. The order is: tap- pull off- hammer on- pull off, and repeat. Practice this slowly and evenly to build coordination before attempting at full speed.

The lead guitar lays out during the mellow bridge section, which gives the song a little space to breath (bars 89-94), and the drums, bass, and rhythm guitar lay down a funky and loose groove. The rhythm guitar plays inversions of A minor and D7 with quick chord stabs followed by chime like sustains (see rhythm guitar transcription). Bars 95-106 feature a modified version of the chorus melody, starting at the 3rd fret position on the low 'E' and 'A' strings and ascending through four octaves, climaxing with a trill on the high 'E' string at the 2oth and 22nd fret. All this is followed by a tremolo lick (bars 103-105) in 3rds, then ascending on the first string using individual notes of E7 and culminating with a 22nd fret bend.

The guitar handles the liquidy fifth solo (bars 107-118) with legato technique. The idea is to pick as few notes as possible, while the left hand uses hammer ons, pull offs, and slides to keep the lick going. Bars 115-117 apply 'octave displacement' to an other wise simple melody to create a twisted and jumpy sound. Dig those huge interval skips!

The sixth solo (bars 119-130) returns to the bluesy stylings of the first two solos, along with plenty of string bending. The solo concludes with triads following the descending chords (Am-G-D/F#-F-E), then drives it home with unison bends over the E7#9 chord.

The Van Halen inspired ending solo (bars 143-146) cuts it up at the 17th fret position with rapid string bending, followed by a quick pentatonic lick incorporating the extended pentatonic box. Use the fourth finger to reach up to the 22nd fret.

WORLD MUSIC JAM

Track 73

by Dave Celentano

Rhythm Guitar

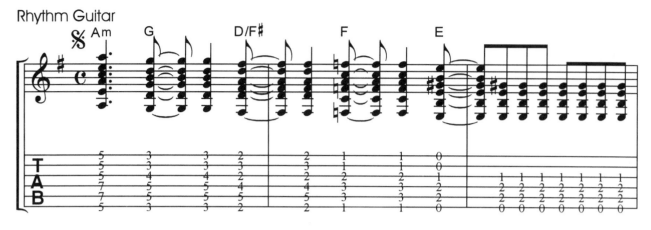

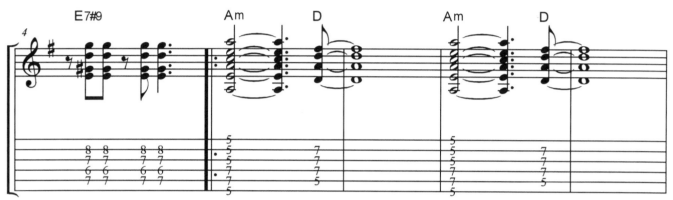

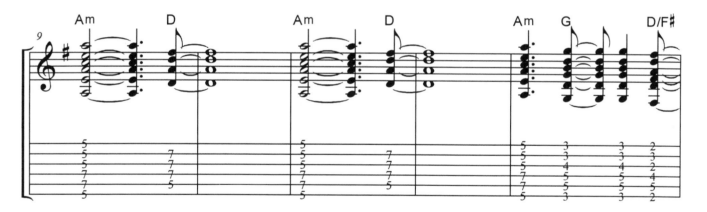

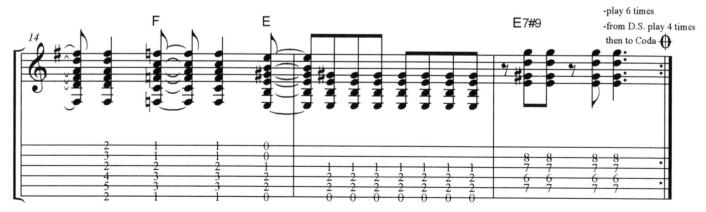

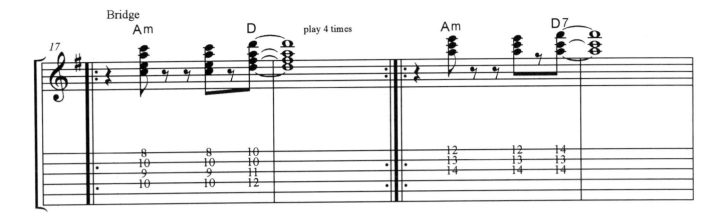

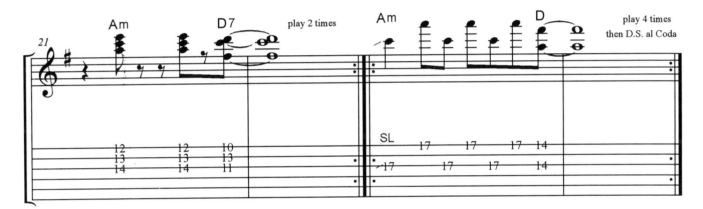

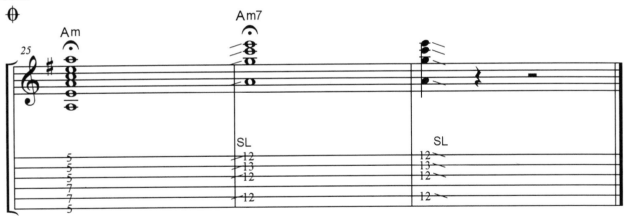

 Coda

67

WORLD MUSIC JAM

Track 73

by Dave Celentano

Lead Guitar Solos

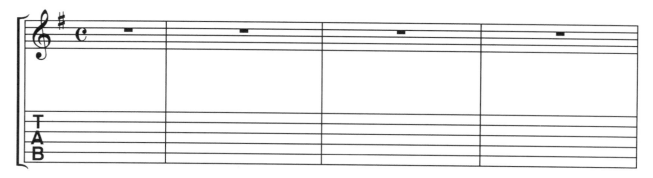

Chorus Melody

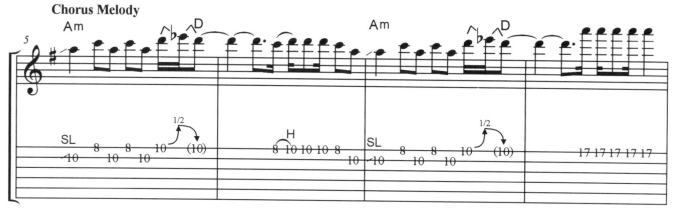

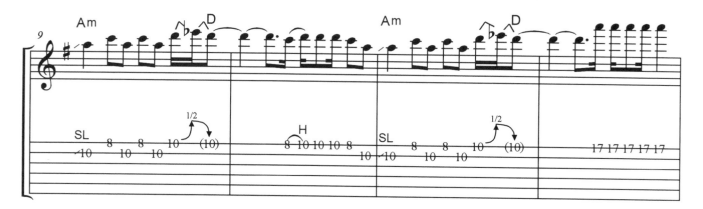

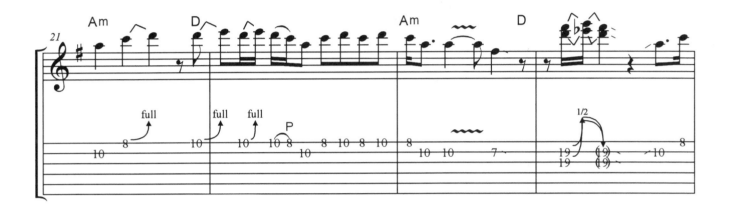

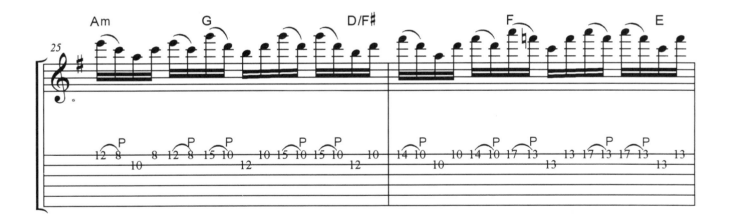

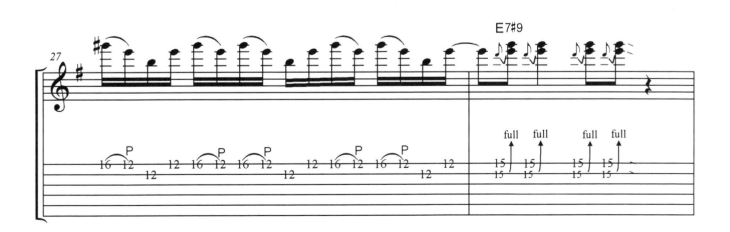

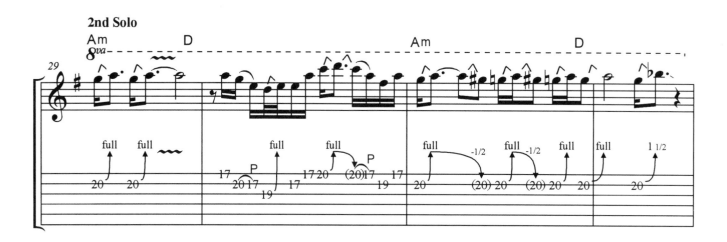

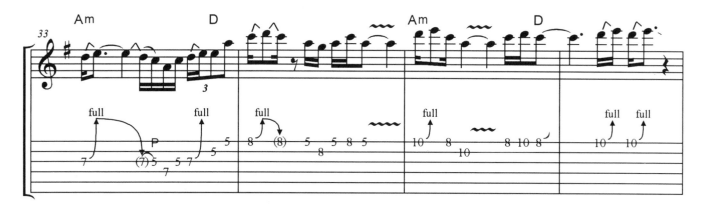

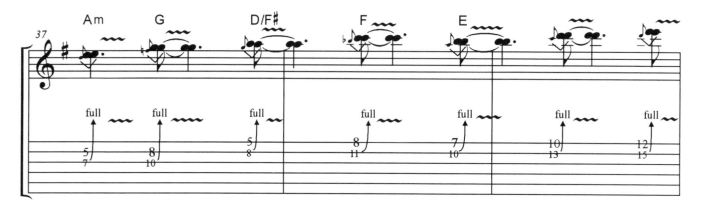

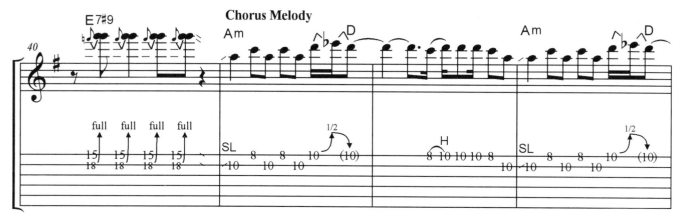

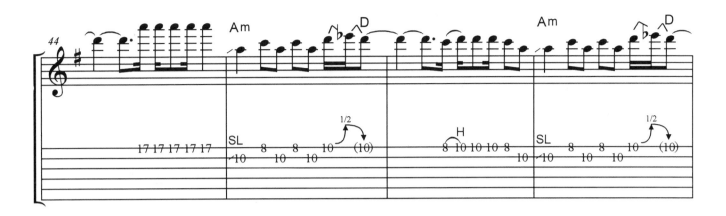

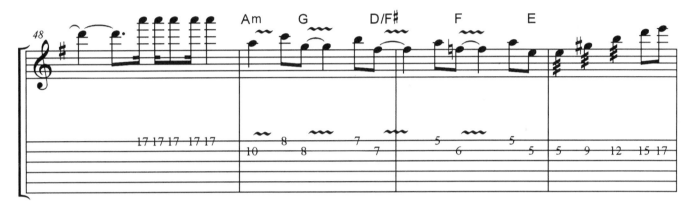

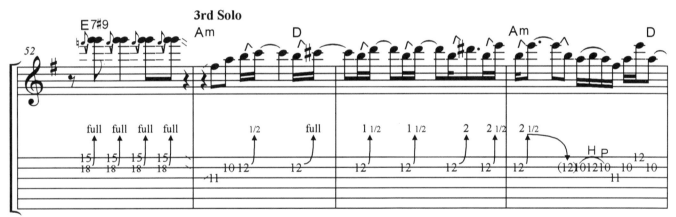

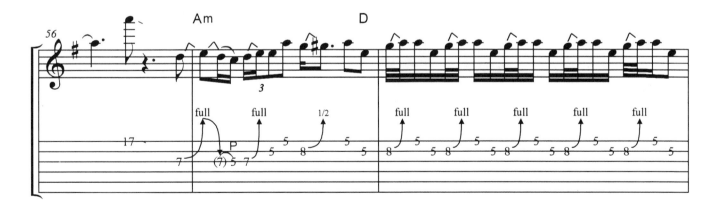

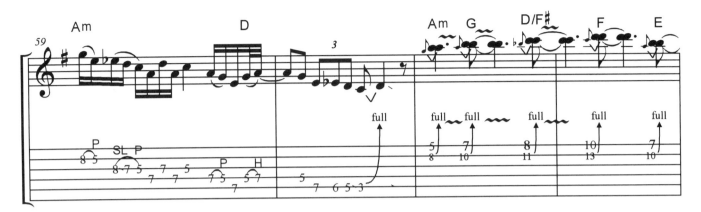

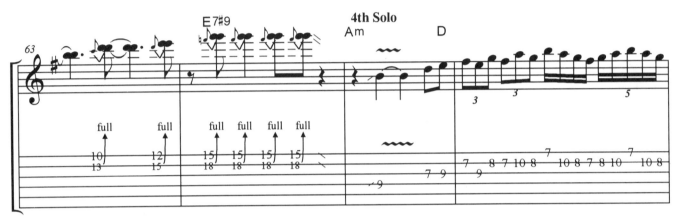

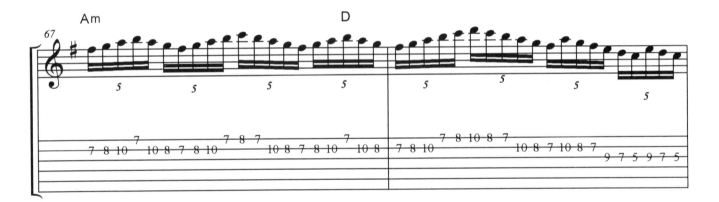

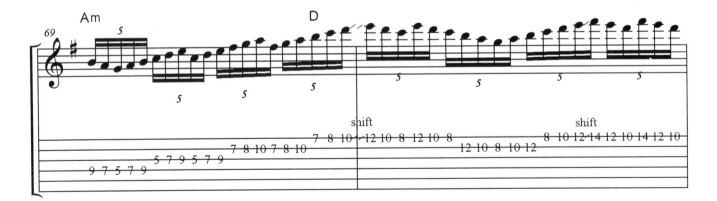

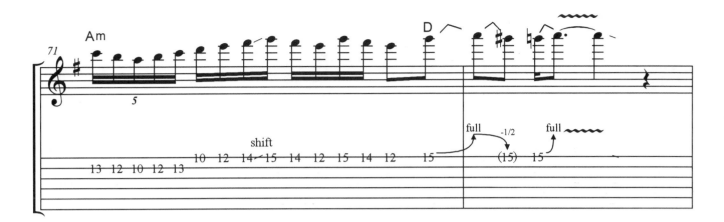

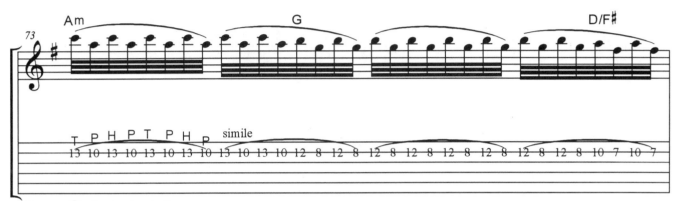

fingers: ① 1 4 1 simile

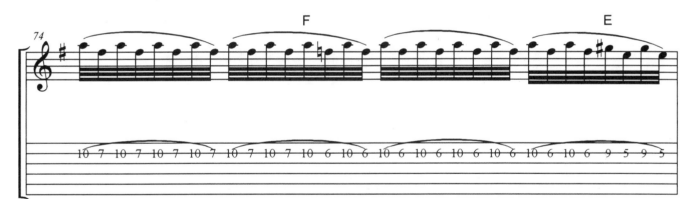

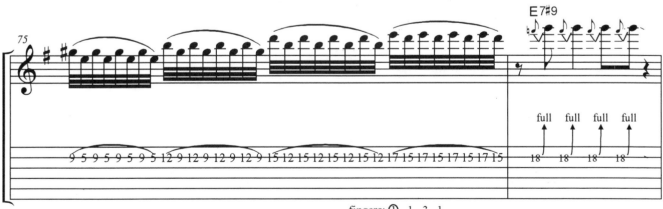

fingers: ① 1 3 1

Chorus Melody

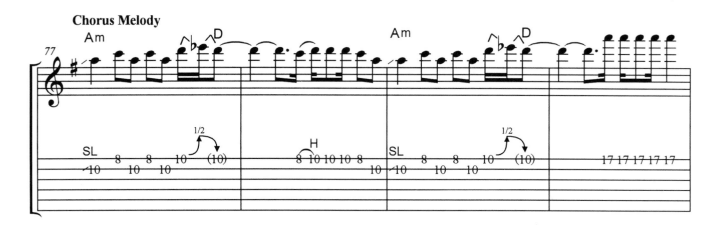

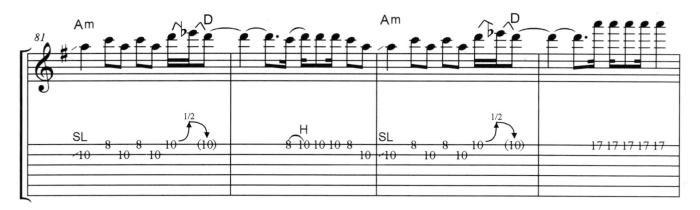

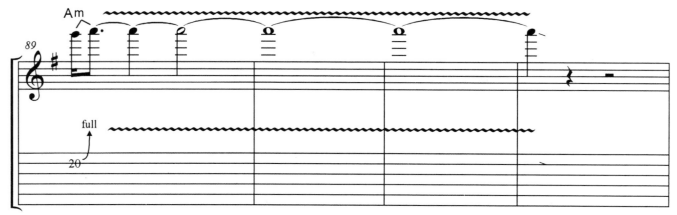

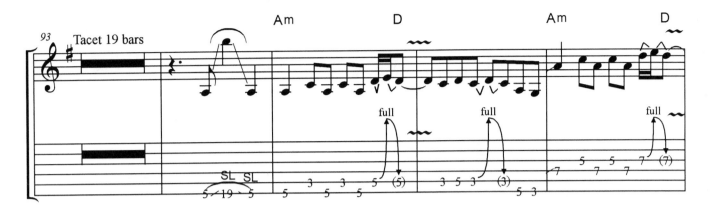

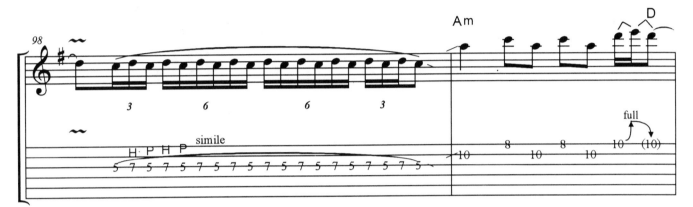

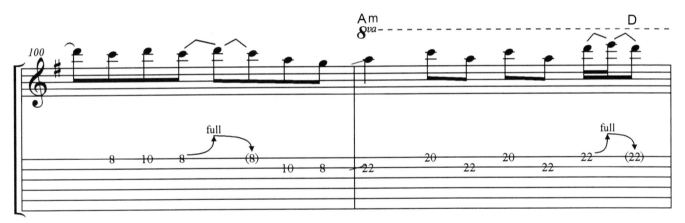

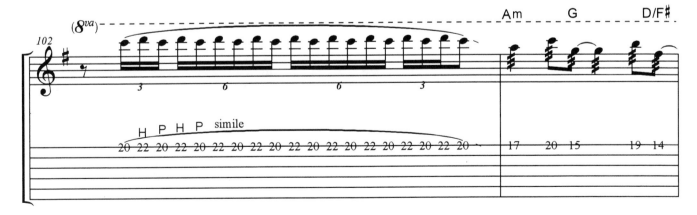

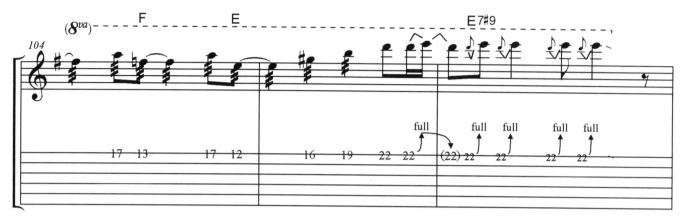

5th Solo

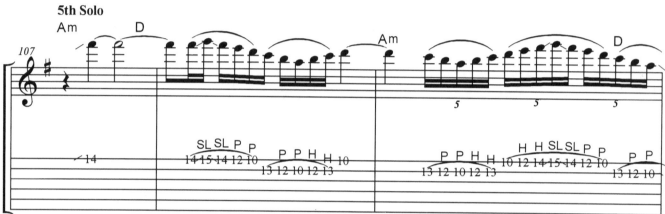

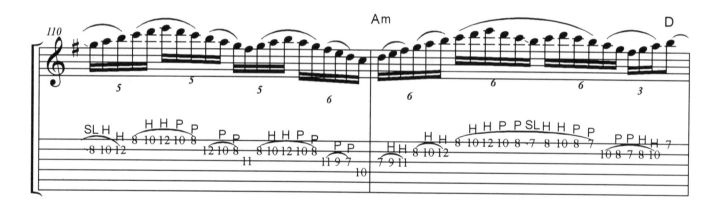

fingers: 4 3 1 2   1 2 3

6th Solo

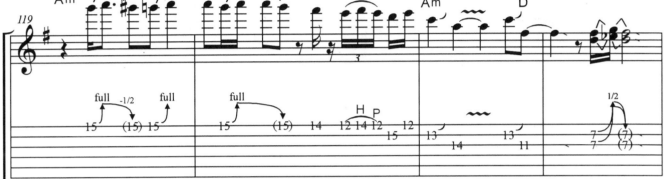

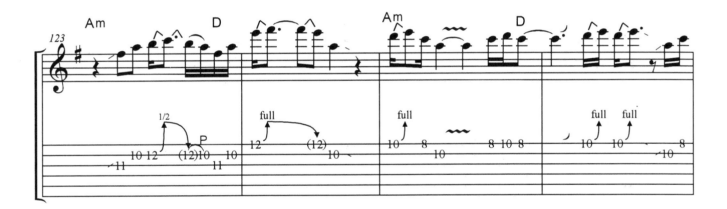

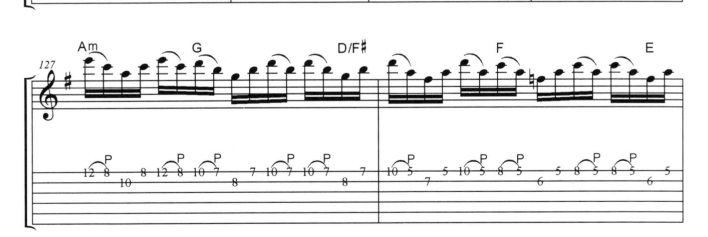

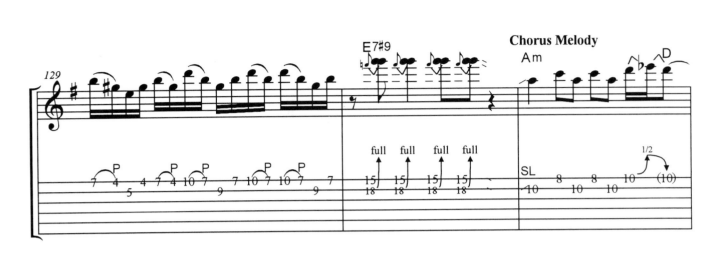
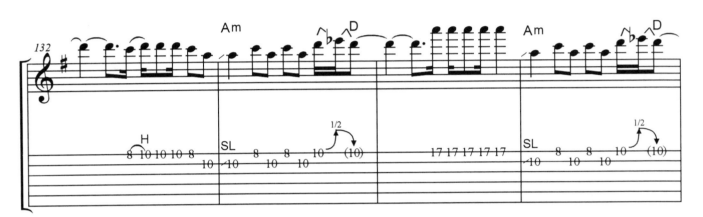
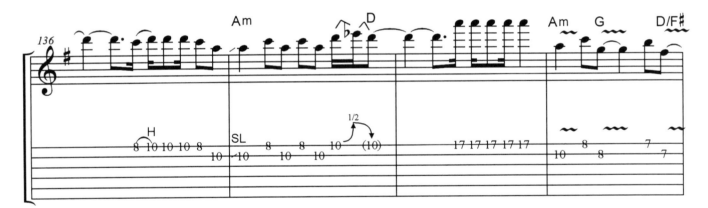

Ending Solo

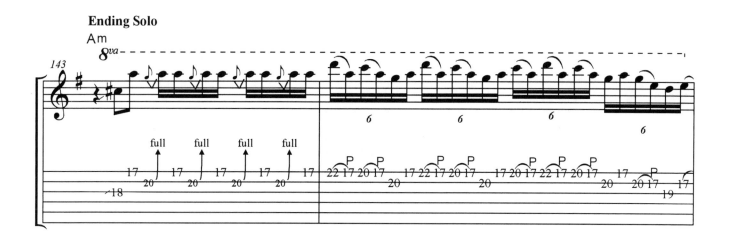

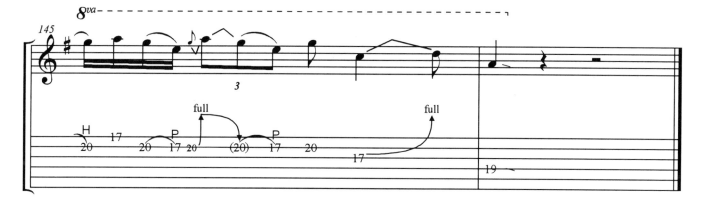

Conclusion

I hope these exercises improve your technique and maybe inspire some new musical ideas of your own. No matter what your goals are on the guitar, you've got to spend time practicing to get results. Playing guitar is like riding a bike- once you learn it correctly, you never forget. Above all, enjoy playing your guitar.

-Dave Celentano

For free information on all Dave Celentano's books, videos, and CDs send a self addressed stamped envelope to:
Flying Fingers Music
P.O. Box 800036
Santa Clarita, CA 91380-0036

Guitar Instruction & Technique from Centerstream Publishing

Guitar Chords Plus
by Ron Middlebrook
A comprehensive study of normal and extended chords, tuning, keys, transposing, capo use, and more. Includes over 500 helpful photos and diagrams, a key to guitar symbols, and a glossary of guitar terms.
00000011..$11.95

Guitar Tuning for the Complete Musical Idiot (For Smart People Too)*
by Ron Middlebrook
A complete book on how to tune up. Contents include: Everything You Need To Know About Tuning; Intonation; Strings; 12-String Tuning; Picks; and much more.
00000002 ....$5.95

Introduction to Roots Guitar

AN OVERVIEW OF NORTH AMERICAN FOLK STYLES
by Doug Cox
This book/CD pack by Canada's premier guitar and Dobro® player introduces beginning to intermediate players to many of the basics of folk/roots guitar. Topics covered include: basic theory, tuning, reading tablature, right- and left-hand patterns, blues rhythms, Travis picking, frailing patterns, flatpicking, open tunings, slide and many more–everything necessary to become a true roots guitar player! The CD includes 40 helpful demonstration tracks.
00000262 Book/CD Pack $17.95
Also available:
00000265 Video..............................$19.95

Killer Pentatonics for Guitar*

by Dave Celentano
Covers innovative and diverse ways of playing pentatonic scales in blues, rock and heavy metal. The licks and ideas in this book will give you a fresh approach to playing the pentatonic scale, hopefully inspiring you to reach for higher levels in your playing. The 37-minute companion CD features recorded examples.
00000285 Book/CD Pack $17.95

Left Hand Guitar Chord Chart*
by Ron Middlebrook
Printed on durable card stock, this "first-of-a-kind" guitar chord chart displays all forms of major and minor chords in two forms, beginner and advanced.
00000005..$2.95

Melody Chords for Guitar*
by Allan Holdsworth
Influential fusion player Allan Holdsworth provides guitarists with a simplified method of learning chords, in diagram form, for playing accompaniments and for playing popular melodies in "chord-solo" style. Covers: major, minor, altered, dominant and diminished scale notes in chord form, with lots of helpful reference tables and diagrams.
00000222..$19.95

Modal Jams and Theory*

USING THE MODES FOR SOLO GUITAR
by Dave Celentano
This book shows you how to play the modes, the theory behind mode construction, how to play any mode in any key, how to play the proper mode over a given chord progression, and how to write chord progressions for each of the seven modes. The accompanying CD includes two rhythm tracks (drums, bass, keyboard and rhythm guitar), and a short solo for each mode so guitarists can practice their solos with a "real" band.
00000163 Book/CD Pack $17.95

Monster Scales and Modes*
by Dave Celentano
This book is a complete compilation of scales, modes, exotic scales, and theory. It covers the most common and exotic scales, theory on how they're constructed, and practical applications. No prior music theory knowledge is necessary, since every section is broken down and explained very clearly.
00000140..$7.95

Open Guitar Tunings*
by Ron Middlebrook
This booklet illustrates over 75 different tunings in easy-to-read diagrams. Includes tunings used by artists such as Chet Atkins, Michael Hedges, Jimmy Page, Joe Satriani and more for rock, blues, bluegrass, folk and country styles including open D (for slide guitar), Em, open C, modal tunings and many more.
00000130..$4.95

Open Tunings for Guitar*

by Dorian Michael
Seasoned guitar vet Dorian Michael provides 14 folk songs in 9 tunings to help guitarists become comfortable with changing tunings to expand their range. Songs are ordered so that changing from one tuning to another is logical and non-intrusive. Includes: Fisher Blues (DADGBE) • Fine Toast to Hewlett (DGDGBE) • George Barbazan (DGDGBD) • Amelia (DGDGCD) • Will the Circle Be Unbroken (DADF#AD) • more.
00000224 Book/CD Pack $19.95

Rock Rhythm Guitar
FOR ACOUSTIC & ELECTRIC GUITAR
by Dave Celentano
In this helpful book/CD pack, ace instructor Dave Celentano cuts out all the confusing technical talk and just gives guitarists the essential tools to get them playing. With his tips, anyone can build a solid foundation of basic skills to play almost any rhythm guitar style. The exercises and examples are all on the CD, and are laid out in order of difficulty, so players can master new techniques, then move on to more challenging material.
00000274 Book/CD Pack $17.95

Scales and Modes in the Beginning*
by Ron Middlebrook
The most comprehensive and complete scale book written especially for the guitar. Chapers include: Fretboard Visualization • Scale Terminology • Scales and Modes • and a Scale to Chord Guide.
00000010 ....$11.95

Slide Guitar and Open Tunings*
by Doug Cox
Explores the basics of open tunings and slide guitar for the intermediate player, including licks, chords, songs and patterns. This is not just a repertoire book, but rather an approach for guitarists to jam with others, invent their own songs, and understand how to find their way around open tunings with and without a slide. The accompanying CD features 37 tracks.
00000243 Book/CD Pack $17.95

Speed Metal
by Dave Celentano
In an attempt to teach the aspiring rock guitarist how to pick faster and play more melodically, Dave Celentano uses heavy metal neo-classical styles from Paganini and Bach to rock in this great new book/CD pack. The book is structured to take the player through the examples in order of difficulty, from easiest to most challenging.
00000261 Book/CD Pack $17.95

*Includes tablature

Centerstream Publishing
P.O. Box 17878 – Anaheim Hills, CA 92817 –p/f 714.779.9390
E-Mail: centerstrm@aol.com   website: centerstream-usa.com